JT's - Volume I

a collection

by Julie Trusler
with daughter Sara Patkin

Farm & Food Publishing
Newton, Iowa

Photography by Curtis Stahr
Design by Sara Patkin and Angie Hoogensen

Printed in the United States of America

First Edition

Library of Congress Control Number: 00-136463
ISBN: 0-9704796-0-3

To two groups of people:

To my family who was willing to try all the "new recipes" I prepared for them year after year.

To the people who came and continue to come to our house year after year.

Without you this book would have remained a dream.

Contents

Introduction..i

Ramblings & Equipment v

First Course 1
    Crab Bisque 2
    Red Pepper & Crab Bisque 3
    Cauliflower Crab Chowder 4
    Cauliflower, Brie & Bacon Soup 4
    Pear Brie Soup..5
    Spinach Soup 6
    Tomato Soup 6
    Soup Under Wraps 7
    French Onion Soup 7
    Chicken Velvet Soup 8
    Tomato Dill Soup 8
    Artichoke Cream Soup 9
    Zucchini Bacon Soup 9
    Smoked Salmon-Filled Rigatoni 10
    Salmon Timbales with Cucumber Sauce 11
    Salmon Napoleons with Beurre Blanc 12
    Timbales of Crab & Spinach Mousse 13
    Crab-Stuffed Mushrooms 14
    Four Cheese & Spinach Tart 15
    Onion Tart..16
    Fried Pasta with Smoked Beef & Sun Dried Tomatoes....17
    Galettes of Dried Beef & Provolone with Fresh Spinach Sauce 18

Salads & Dressings 19
    Greens with Jack Cheese & Toasted Walnuts with Shallot Vinaigrette 20
    Hearts of Palm Salad..21
    Semi-Caesar Salad 22
    Romaine, Mandarin Orange & Glazed Almonds Salad....23
    Strawberry & Green Salad with Sweet Garlic Dressing 24
    Greens & Strawberries with Poppy Seed Dressing 25
    Spinach & Vegetable Salad with Chutney Dressing 26
    Spinach Bacon Salad 27
    Broccoli, Bacon & Raisin Salad 28
    Cauliflower Bacon Salad 28
    Hearts of Palm & Black Bean Salad 29
    Fresh Mushroom Salad 30
    Red Cabbage Salad 30
    Sauerkraut Salad 31
    Wilted Cabbage Salad 31
    Pasta Salad with Mustard Dressing 32
    Dill Pasta Vegetable Salad 33
    Sweet Pasta Salad 33
    Potato Salad 34
    Surprise Combination Salad 35
    Creamy Cole Slaw Dressing.................................35
    Strawberry Vinaigrette 36
    Raspberry Vinaigrette...36

Main Dish 37
    Beef Tenderloin with Mustard Balsamic Vinegar Sauce 38
    Beef with Wine Sauce 39
    Five Hour Stew 40
    Stove Top Casserole 40
    Cheesy Taco Casserole 41
    Tex-Italian Pasta Fiesta 42
    Marinated Pork Tenderloin Medallions with Ginger Mayonnaise 43
    Pork Tenderloin Tournedos 44
    Sauces for Pork Tenderloin 45
    Cornish Hen with Sausage & Mushroom Stuffing 46
    Seafood Casserole 47
    Gâteau Florentine 48
    Stuffed Chicken Breast Basics 50
    Chicken Fromage 51
    Chicken with Herb & Garlic Cheese 52
    Chicken with Pastrami, Spinach & Cheese 53
    Spinach-Stuffed Chicken 54
    Chicken with Sun Dried Tomatoes & Mushrooms 55
    Crab-Stuffed Chicken Breasts 56
    Chicken with Raspberry Vinegar Sauce 57
    Chicken in Phyllo with Cream Sauce 58
    Chicken in Phyllo with Lemon & Green Onion Sauce 59
    Chicken in Puff Pastry 60
    Fiesta Chicken & Fiesta Chicken Casserole 61
    Chicken Casserole 62
    Ham & Chicken Cannelloni 63
    Ham & Chicken Bake with Artichokes 64
    Creamy Pasta with Ham & Broccoli 65
    Ham, Broccoli & Rice Casserole 66
    Egg Casserole 67
    B.O.O.M. Quiche 68

Bread, Pasta & Rice 69
    Crescent Rolls & Cinnamon Twist Danish 70
    Overnight Coffeecake 71
    Sticky Cinnamon Rolls, Cinnamon Bread & Cocktail Buns 72
    Rye–Carrot Bread 74
    Crunchy Bread 75
    Pull-Apart Cheese Bread 75
    Rotini in Red Butter Sauce 76
    Pasta and Vegetables in Garlic Sauce 76
    Pasta Shells with Three Cheeses 77
    French Rice 78
    Brown Rice with Mushrooms, Sour Cream & Jack Cheese 78
    Green Bean & Almond Rice 79
    Rice with Dried Cranberries, Green Onions & Pine Nuts 80
    Barley Casserole 80

Photographs 81

Vegetables 97

Sweet & Sour Carrots 98
Baby Carrots with Mustard & Brown Sugar Glaze 98
Carrots & Apricots 99
Carrot & Apple Purée 99
Julienne Vegetables with Lemon Butter Sauce 100
Rainbow of Four Vegetables with Hollandaise Sauce 101
Norwegian Stir-Fry Broccoli & Carrots....................102
Broccoli with Orange Shallot Butter 103
Peas with Broccoli Medallions 104
Country French Peas 104
Snappy Green Beans 105
Onion Fritters 105
Spinach-Stuffed Onions 106
Spinach Strudel 107
Scrambled Cabbage............................108
Creamy Cabbage Packets with Bacon & Onion 109
South of the Border Squash 110
Sweet & Yummy Corn Pudding.....................110
Sweet Potato, Peach & Cashew Bake 111
Julienne Potatoes..............................111
Cheesy Potatoes...............................112
Diced Potatoes with Bacon Cream 112
Oven Roasted Potatoes 113
"Parmesan" Potatoes...........................113
Twice-Baked Potatoes 114

Desserts 115

Graham Cracker Crust 116
Basic Pie Crust 116
Chocolate Hazelnut Torte 117
Basic Chocolate Cake 118
Devil's Mousse Cake with Crème de Cacao Cream 119
Chocolate Praline Cake 120
Warm Chocolate Cake with a Soft Heart.................121
"Caramel" Sauce 121
Tin Roof Tart.................................122
Tin Roof Tart II 123
Chocolate Crème Brûlée 124
Butterscotch Crème Brûlée 125
Raspberry Crème Brûlée.........................126
Crème Caramel 127
Cheesecake Basics.............................128
Sour Cream Cheesecake 129
Creamy Raspberry Swirl Cheesecake 130
Raspberry or Blackberry Purée 130
Blackberry Cheesecake 131
Chocolate Marble Cheesecake......................132
Lemon Curd Cheesecake.........................133
Lemon Curd 133
Meringue Pie Shell 134

White Chocolate Strawberry Filling for Meringue Pie Shell 134
Lemon Filling for Meringue Pie Shell 135
Chocolate Toffee Filling for Meringue Pie Shell 135
Strawberry Cream Pie 136
Pecan Cream Pie 137
Pumpkin Layer Pie 138
Lemon Layer Pie 139
Classic Bavarian Cream 140
Toasted Almond Bavarian with Raspberry Sauce 140
Chocolate Marble Bavarian Pie 141
Puff Pastry Pears 142
Strawberry Tart 143
Peach Praline Angel Cake 144
Easy Fruit Cobbler 144
Cherry Crisp 145
Apricot & Cream Sponge Layer Cake 146
Apricot Purée 147
Quick Pastry Cream 147
Cream Puff Filling 147
Jelly Roll 148
Carrot Cake 149
Marble Bundt Cake 150
Cream-Filled Cupcakes 151
Napoleon Creams 152
Cookie Dough Brownies 153
Peanut Butter Cookies 154
Molasses Crisps 154
Chocolate Chip Cookies 155
Cranberry Toffee Oatmeal Cookies 155
Almond Crescents 156
Buckeyes 156
Eskimo Balls 157
Salted Nut Bars 157
Scroll Butter Cookies 158
Oatmeal Shortbread 159
Lace Oatmeal Cookies 159
Chocolate Mint Bars 160

Miscellaneous **161**
Popcorn Balls 162
Sorbet 162
Crusty Chicken Wings 163
Cardinal Victory Punch 163
Guacamole 164
Guacamole Pie 164
Ham Salad 165
Radish Butter 165

About the Author **167**

Sources **168**

Index **169**

Introduction

Golden brown outside, soft and hot inside oven roast potatoes; fresh asparagus with brown butter and lemon; a juicy medium rare hamburger or the first bite of pecan cream pie – this is why I cook. I love to eat! The challenge and the process of producing a product that is just right also fuels the fire. I never get bored chasing that illusive "perfection."

Knowing why I cook does not answer the question "Why a cookbook?" Every time I spend thirty minutes looking for a recipe or when I wake up in a cold sweat dreaming about a fire that destroyed all my recipes it sounds like a good idea. Then I think about how I cook: Whipping cream is the beverage of choice, butter is purchased by the case and there is no such thing as too much cheese. Who would want my recipes? With the help of my family, we decided to find out.

We decided to record the recipes we use in the business with only a few of our family recipes added so the kids would have them. The recipes come from everywhere. As I collected the recipes over the years, I tried to document the source. In most cases we were able to include the "inspiration" for each recipe. Documenting gives you a history. Recipes from family and friends provide not only some of the best recipes but also memories that come alive every time you prepare the dish. I talk about some of those memories in the book. If a publication was the source of the recipe, you begin to see which ones are more helpful for your way of cooking and also how well the recipe holds up over time. Sometimes it leaves you with a mystery. The B.O.O.M. Quiche recipe comes from the *San Diego Home and Garden*. I've never been to San Diego and I've never subscribed to the *San Diego Home and Garden*! Of course there is no substitute for a good general library including basic cookbooks like *Joy of Cooking, Better Homes and Gardens*, Betty Crocker and Julia Child's books. I still use these books all the time and they show the wear.

The first step was to record the recipe as I really cooked it. As you know, you start with a basic recipe and you tweak it here and there until it tastes right to you. I tried very hard to record my tweaking. For some ingredients, I include the brand name because that is the way I make it. The other brands don't taste the same, not wrong, just different, therefore the recipe wouldn't taste the way you had it at our house. Then our girls pitched in and began to test the recipes as I had written them. Karlene even had tasting parties and invited her friends to critique the recipes. Karlene is a less experienced cook so she was a good tester and her friends were very good sports and tasted, evaluated and suggested. Sara and Mari also did many hours of testing and found some interesting omissions and additions. We had friends test the recipes to see if they could understand the directions to make the recipe successfully. Everyone was so helpful and conscientious about helping. It was wonderful.

Once the recipes were in working order, we had to decide if we wanted pictures. Everyone wanted pictures with every recipe! We decided on a <u>section</u> of pictures. Most of the pictures show the finished recipe, but a few are there to help prepare the recipe, namely the Crescent and Cinnamon Twist Danish recipe because it shows the dough folding method and the Salmon Napoleon recipe because it shows how easy this recipe is to make.

If you are lucky in life, with everything you do you learn. Well we learned about photo sessions! We had no idea what was going to happen and how fast everything had to be ready. Sara was setting up the shot, I was making the food and Karlene was taking the food back and forth from the kitchen to the photo set up in the dining room. In three and one-half hours, we did ten shots. We were exhausted and the kitchen was destroyed. Curt, our photographer, walked into the kitchen and took a picture, he couldn't help himself. He kept saying "I just can't believe this!" I never asked him what he meant, but you can see the picture on page 96. The second photo shoot went much better, even Curt thought so.

With recipes and pictures in hand, we then moved on to formatting, paper choice, binding and cover design. It's been an exciting, wonderful experience. I have had so many good laughs working on this project with my family and have met some great people I wouldn't otherwise have known.

Special thanks needs to be extended to our daughter Sara. She has been the driving force from the beginning. She is the one who actually made the book a reality by using her computer skills and giving her valuable time. To me, she is a wonder woman the way she can work the computer.

My family has tried many new recipes over the years and most of the time they could eat them, but I don't count it as a good recipe until I find out if they would be happy if I made the recipe again. I hope your family and friends will be happy when you make a recipe from this book the <u>second</u> time.

A Treasure

Completing this cookbook is an impressive accomplishment for our mother. It is also a valuable service for her customers who have been requesting it for years. But the book has special meaning for us, as in many ways it represents our childhood. It is filled with memories of Mom, of working in the restaurant, of trying recipes and of being together.

Mom began her business as a way to stay home with us while earning income. It also allowed us to work with her in the restaurant where we gained valuable experience and earned some money. This kept our family together more and created some unique discussion opportunities.

We all have memories of growing up with the restaurant. It may surprise you to know that Sara woke up feeling nauseous every morning from smelling rolls. None of us knew this until Mom started writing this cookbook! Although that's a small sacrifice because when Mom was selling rolls we never had to ride the bus to school because there was always an order to be delivered.

Darren will never forget the night when he was working and a famous professional basketball player came for dinner. (He will remain nameless but he played for the Chicago Bulls.) He was incredibly nice to Darren who was then a new teenager. He showed Darren his championship ring and gave him an autograph. Darren also had the privilege of working when *The Des Moines Register* restaurant critic came to eat and he received a very favorable review.

Both Karlene and Mari have wonderful, countless, memories of how our friends (mostly boys) would come over, night after night, and wait in the wings for leftover food. They would usually come on nights we were working, but some felt so comfortable at our house they would even come when we weren't there! Mom always loved to have kids around the house, the more the merrier. There was always food to share.

We also learned some valuable skills while working in the restaurant. We all know how to correctly set a table for a five-course meal and we know proper etiquette for formal dining. Because of our experience, we thought this was common knowledge. Now that we are adults, we've learned this is not the case. Even without the restaurant we would likely have learned about table etiquette because it is important to Mom. We've also learned a great deal about tipping!

One thing we didn't learn while we were living at home is how to cook. Many people find this surprising, but it is true. When you have a master chef in the kitchen, why disturb a good thing! It's not that Mom didn't try, but until we were on our own, we didn't internalize all the things she taught us. Most of our training has come over the phone since we left the house. We are all turning out to be good cooks (although Darren isn't exactly on the map yet), thanks to Mom and to her amazing recipes.

Mom has said repeatedly that this cookbook is for us so we can have the recipes we remember while growing up written down in one place. In many ways she's right. Although we have no doubt this cookbook will be widely enjoyed, we will be the ones who treasure it. Thanks, Mom!

Your Children
Mari, Sara, Karlene and Darren

Julie's Ramblings

Toasted nuts: I have decided most nuts are infinitely better if they are toasted. That includes almonds, walnuts, pecans and you already know about peanuts. The easiest way to toast them is in the oven. Bake on a cookie sheet in one layer at 350 degrees for 10-15 minutes until the nuts are lightly brown and they smell terrific. Do not chop before toasting. Chopping makes too many different size pieces that toast at different times so some are burned before others are toasted. Cool them, put in a plastic bag and store in the freezer.

Washing greens: I'm sure you all have your favorite method for this. I'm not particularly fond of bitter greens so I cut the greens in bite size pieces first then I wash and rinse them. This rinses off some of the bitter juices.

Cutting vs. tearing greens: I've never been convinced that tearing the greens is the best method. It is time consuming, the pieces are very large and hard to eat and pulling the leaves bruises them much more than a nice sharp knife. I've read that the knife discolors the leaves. Unless you are using an old rusty carbon steel knife, I don't think that is true. Lettuce, especially iceberg lettuce discolors from exposure to the air. So cut away with my blessing!

Soup bases (broths): You're going to see references to soup base or broth in the book only about a million times! I use them for everything. One of the best ingredients I found because of the restaurant business is a good quality soup base. When a recipe says chicken broth, for instance, I use soup base plus water to make the broth. There are many soup bases, but the ones I use are from the AJ Minor Company. These are available to the home cook by mail. The address is listed in the back of the book, page 168. They come in many flavors and they freeze for long-term storage.

Eggs: One of my favorite things. They do so many things. When I run out of eggs I can't think of anything to make that doesn't have egg in it. I always use extra large eggs. I just think they are a better deal. In our market they generally are only 1 or 2 cents more than large eggs. The truth is they aren't that much bigger – I measured 3 large eggs and 3 extra large eggs and there was only about 1 tablespoon more volume with the extra large eggs. One dozen large eggs weigh 24-27 ounces. One dozen extra large eggs weigh 27-30 ounces. I still like extra large, besides they fill the carton better than large eggs. Just shake a carton of large and a carton of extra large and hear the difference! Remember in all the recipes in this book I use extra large eggs. Now one more note. We have all heard the warnings against eating raw eggs. So far I have not been worried about the risk. There are many recipes in this book that use raw egg whites for meringues, etc. You decide if you want to use the recipe. As time goes by pasteurized eggs will be more available in the market and they can then be used for such recipes. Until then, the choice is yours. Just be careful.

Mayonnaise: Hard as it is to believe I didn't grow up with a heritage for mayonnaise, we always used the creamy salad dressing type spread (i.e. Miracle Whip). When I started to branch out and learn about mayonnaise I found people are very passionate about their choice and I too have very strong feelings about it. For my taste and the one I use in the recipes I choose Kraft Mayonnaise. So if you are in the Hellmann's camp you might like the recipes better with that flavor. There is a difference.

Thickening methods: This is major. Learning the different ways to thicken soups and sauces can make your cooking experience. I'm going to talk about 3 ways to thicken liquids. 1) Flour and fat (butter, margarine, oil). You all have done this – you melt the butter in a pan and add an equal amount of flour (this is called a roux). Cook the roux a little bit then add the liquid and bring it to a boil to thicken. A note about the liquid. I have the best luck adding most of the liquid all at once and I like the liquid to be cold. I get the best results this way. Cold liquid to hot roux. However, I watch many cooking shows and each chef has his/her own way. Emmeril says cold liquid and Sara Moulton says hot liquid. Go figure. 2) Flour and fat – part 2. In this method mix equal parts softened butter or margarine and flour in a bowl (this is called beurie manie). You add this a little at a time to hot liquid to thicken it. With this method you can thicken something without adding extra liquid. This beurre manie can be kept wrapped up in plastic wrap in the refrigerator for quick access. 3) Slurry. Equal parts cornstarch or flour and cold water. Cornstarch mixes easier with water but flour does work. Use a whisk to get it smooth. Add the slurry to simmering liquid then bring to a boil to thicken. Cornstarch will make a clear sauce compared to flour and it will also take less cornstarch to get the same thickness as flour. Generally speaking, cornstarch thickens with half as much as flour. The slurry is fast and if you add it carefully you can control the thickness of your sauce.

Romano vs. Parmesan cheese: When I first started cooking most of the recipes used Parmesan cheese and it was more available than Romano. Well, I didn't like it that much. Part of the reason was the cheese I used wasn't very good. I was lucky enough to find an Italian grocery store that had wonderful owners who helped me with many things Italian that I didn't know about. I mentioned to them that I didn't like Parmesan that much so she suggested trying Romano instead. I really like it much better so whenever Parmesan was used I substituted Romano. In my menus for the business, I just left the word Parmesan because I thought people were more familiar with it and would have a better idea of the flavor they were ordering. As the years have gone by I think now I could tell them they were ordering Romano and they would know what flavor to expect. So that is why I use so much Romano in my recipes.

Cheese: I'm of the "a little more cheese is better than a little less" school of cheese measuring. I've never quite figured out how they measure 1 cup shredded cheese. I go by ounces. 1 cup = 4 ounces. I look at the package and see how many ounces in the whole package and then cut off the amount I think is close to what I need. Of course a scale is a handy tool to have for this. This works on most cheeses except the finely grated hard cheeses such as Parmesan or Romano. Then I use a measuring cup patting it down just a little.

Lemon juice: When I started cooking for other people I decided to trust my own judgment and use the ingredients that tasted the best to me and try not to be told by someone else what was best. Fresh lemon juice was one of the things I had to use. The stuff in the jar just doesn't taste or smell right to me. Anytime you see lemon juice in a recipe it means fresh.

Flour: If the recipe says flour, I use regular bleached all-purpose flour. There are a few recipes that use cake flour and that is what I recommend. Unless the recipe says sift then measure I use the "spoon lightly" method. That is – fluff up the flour a bit and then lightly spoon into a measuring cup then take a straight edge and level off the top. Yes, I really do this for cakes, cookies and desserts – however bread is not quite so exact and I dip the cup and come pretty close!

Butter vs. margarine: Ten or maybe even five years ago I wouldn't have such a definite opinion about the difference in baking. In the last few years margarine has changed – they don't even call it margarine anymore – it's vegetable spread. That's because to call it margarine it needs to have 80% oil in it. When I last checked the margarine package I use, it was down to 65%. This makes a difference in baking. Another problem is the smell of some margarines. I don't know what butter they were smelling when they decided to put butter flavor in margarine but it doesn't smell like any butter I've ever smelled. I have written the company and complained but I'm just one voice. There is a place for the lower fat spreads but not in baking. Give us a choice. Enough! So I use a lot more butter in baking than I used to. I also use some solid vegetable shortening in breads and some cookies but not that butter-flavored stuff.

Cutting bacon: I know this might sound strange to talk about cutting bacon but I think it makes a difference in the texture if you dice it or julienne the bacon. First of all, lets hope we are all talking about the same bacon – I'm talking about the 1 pound packages that come with about 12-15 slices overlapping. I prefer the thin sliced, but that's personal. When the recipe calls for diced bacon start with cold bacon, open the package and cut across the slices in $1/4$-inch pieces – don't cut one slice at a time. If the recipe calls for julienne slices start with partially frozen bacon (30 minutes in the freezer), open the package and, cutting all the slices at one time, make 4 crosswise cuts (across the slices). Then take each section and cut small $1/4$-inch or less strips the opposite direction – that is with the length of the slice. If it is cold enough this is not hard to do. With both diced and julienne, put the whole mess of pieces in a frying pan and stir over high heat to fry, separating and stirring at the same time, to the desired crispness.

Salt: I use it! I know that is not politically correct but it makes things taste better. Salt has become complicated – kosher salt, sea salt, iodized salt, etc., etc., etc. What do you use? When I was growing up in the Midwest, we were encouraged to use iodized salt to prevent goiters from a lack of iodine in the diet. I don't know when I've heard anyone talk about iodine in the diet or the lack thereof, but secretly I'm afraid of a goiter popping out of my neck so I use iodized salt and kosher salt. Another factor to watch for is sodium content. It can vary with the salt. I've heard of salt with 280 mg. of sodium per $1/4$ teaspoon to 540 mg. sodium per $1/4$ teaspoon. Check your label, especially if you are using a new salt.

Pepper: I don't use it! Well, I don't use it as a standard seasoning for meat, soup, vegetables, casseroles, etc. So if you try a recipe and you normally season with pepper you might think it is missing something. Just do it – add it to your taste. I'm slowly learning to use pepper so there are a few recipes that call for pepper.

Meat seasoning: In the last year or so, I've noticed some meats have been flavor enhanced with what is basically a salt solution. Although this does tenderize and flavor the meat, it leaves little option as far as salt is concerned because it is very salty. Check your labels before adding any salt to meat - especially pork tenderloin and chicken breast.

Equipment & Helpful Tools

Right up front you need to know that I like equipment and gadgets. A lot of time is spent in the kitchen and anything that makes it more fun or take less time seems like a good idea.

Good pots and pans are a must. You will see the phrase "heavy saucepan" used over and over in this book. A "heavy saucepan" should be a good even conductor of heat. Aluminum is the most affordable good conductor. A pan made with thick aluminum is a good pan, however, unprotected aluminum will react with certain acidic foods. If the aluminum is anodized or encased in stainless steel it makes a good pan a great pan. There are several brands with a wide range of prices on the market. There are very good pans in the mid-price range and of course the very expensive pans do a good job. I've cooked a lot of food using mid-price pans.

A free-standing mixer has always been a part of my cooking experience and therefore it seems indispensible to me. I know for sure it makes baking more fun and less work. Trying to make a meringue pie shell or angel food cake without a free-standing mixer takes dedication and a strong arm. A mixer makes easy work of cookie dough, whipped cream and bread dough, all with hands free. If you have the space, think about getting a free-standing mixer.

Although food processors have been in the food industry for a long time, they have really made their mark in the home kitchen in the last 20 years. With a little practice, you can chop and slice large quantities of food in a very short time. It has made dishes that require a very smooth texture such as salmon mousse very easy for the home cook. There are some recipes in this book such as "Sweet and Sour Carrots," you won't want to try without the shredding disc and it's worth its weight in gold if you have to shred a large quantity of cheese. Once you learn how to make a pie crust with a processor, you'll wonder how you made it any other way! I use both the mixer and the food processor every day, but then I cook all day! If there has to be a choice made between a mixer or a processor, I think you will get more day-to-day use out of a processor.

For years I've been on a crusade to acquaint everyone with cooking parchment. It can truly change your life - well at least your baking life! It is a silicon-coated paper that prevents sticking when used in baking. I use it for almost everything I put in the oven. It's great for cookies, cakes and rolls, but I also use it under chicken dishes, savory pastries and even vegetables such as "Parmesan" Potatoes. You can get it at most kitchen stores, but it is also available through mail order catalogs. Sources are mentioned on page 168.

Some other things you can put on your wish list that are invaluable to me are a fine mesh strainer for very smooth custard or removing seeds, a pastry cloth for easy-rolling pastry or making rolls, an instant-read thermometer for breads and meats, and 5-ounce custard cups or ramekins for crème brûlée, crème caramel and other individually served dishes.

The key to getting the most use out of your equipment is to have it easily accessible. That might mean sacrificing some counter space for a utensil holder or a food processor. Another thing I've found very useful is to have more than one of certain things like rubber scrapers, measuring spoons and cups and even can openers. Having a second can opener on the other side of the kitchen makes it easy for someone to help without interrupting you at your work space.

As I said, I like gadgets and they are always coming up with something new. Right now I'm finding many uses for the heat resistant silicone scrapers. I'm going to have to make room on my counter! Just remember sometimes everything can get dirty at the same time, see page 96.

First Course

soup, fish & pastries

Crab Bisque

8 cups

Instead of adding the crabmeat to the saucepan, you can distribute it evenly among individual soup bowls so that each person has an equal amount of crab.

Inspiration: This comes from a crab dip recipe given to me by Dorothy Forsythe who got it from Lou Ankeny, both friends.

½	cup butter or margarine
2	bunches green onions, sliced using some of the green (about ¾ cup total)
2	large stalks celery, finely chopped
½	cup flour
4	cups liquid (chicken broth, clam juice, crab soup base, or a combination)
1	(10 ¾-ounce) can cream of shrimp soup
1½	cups heavy cream
1	tablespoon fresh lemon juice, or to taste
¼	teaspoon garlic powder, or to taste
1	(6-ounce) can crabmeat, drained (you may need to remove some cartiledge)

In large saucepan over medium high heat, melt butter. Add onions and celery and sauté until vegetables are soft, about 4 minutes. Add flour and stir to blend. Add liquid and bring to a boil, stirring constantly. Reduce heat to low, add soup and cream and continue heating until soup is smooth and hot. Add lemon juice and garlic powder. Add crabmeat and stir.

The liquid choice is difficult because I use a combination of crab soup base and clam soup base from a restaurant supply warehouse. I have seen them in gourmet food shops, but not very often. That is why I suggest clam juice or chicken broth or you could even use fish bouillon cubes. Check for seasoning before you serve in case you need additional salt.

Red Pepper & Crab Bisque

I love this — great color, great taste and you can reduce or omit the cream for a low-fat choice.

4	tablespoons butter
1½	cups chopped onion
1½	cups chopped celery
2	cups chopped red pepper (2-3 peppers)
1½	teaspoons Old Bay Seasoning
6	cups fish stock, clam juice or chicken broth (or a combination)
1½	cups diced russet potatoes (1-2 potatoes)*
1	cup heavy cream
1	(6-ounce) can crab, or more to taste (lump crab is the most elegant, but it is hard to find in our area)

Melt butter in heavy 2½-3 quart saucepan over low heat. Add onion, celery, red pepper and seasoning. Cover and cook 10 minutes, stirring twice. (This smells so great!) Add stock and potatoes, bring to a boil. Reduce heat, cover and simmer until potatoes are very tender (about 30 minutes). Working in batches, purée soup in a blender (fill blender only ⅓ full at a time and put a towel over the lid when blending because the liquid is very hot and could spit out). Return to saucepan, add cream and heat to serving temperature. Check for seasoning. Distribute crab among individual soup bowls and ladle soup on top.

8 cups

~

*Be sure to use russet potatoes because they have the most starch. The potato is used to thicken this soup.

~

Inspiration:
Bon Appétit, 1993

Cauliflower Crab Chowder

Don't be put off by the combination – you'll love it!

3-4	cups small bite-size cauliflower florets
$1/2$	cup butter or margarine
$1/2$	cup flour
2	cups chicken broth
1	cup heavy cream
8	ounces soft cream cheese with onion & chive
$1/4$	cup vermouth
2	ounces chopped pimiento
6	ounces crab or more if you like crab

Put cauliflower pieces in a $1\,1/2$-quart saucepan and barely cover with water (about 2 cups). Cover and cook just until cauliflower is crisp-tender (4-6 minutes). Remove from heat, do not drain. Set aside.

In a $2\,1/2$-3-quart saucepan or larger, over medium heat melt butter. Add flour and cook about 1 minute. Add chicken broth and bring to a boil, then reduce heat. Add cauliflower with its cooking liquid. Then add remaining ingredients except crab. Stir to melt cheese. Check for salt.

If you know how many servings you are going to have, you can distribute the crab evenly among the bowls. Then ladle the soup on top. If not, just add the crab to the soup and serve.

I really like to use lump crab but it is very hard to find in our area so just use the best you can find.

8 cups

The base of this soup is chicken broth, so if you have someone who is allergic to crab, it is very easy to give them the same soup without the crab and it still tastes great.

Inspiration: *Better Homes & Gardens*, 1997

Cauliflower, Brie & Bacon Soup

$1/2$	pound bacon, chopped
2	medium onions, chopped (2-3 cups)
1	head cauliflower, separated into florets (about 4 cups)
3	cups chicken broth
2	cans (10 $3/4$-ounce) cream of celery soup
8	ounces Brie cheese, cut in pieces or 5 ounces spreadable Brie
	salt and/or hot pepper sauce to taste

In a large saucepan, fry bacon until brown and beginning to crisp. Drain, reserving 2 tablespoons drippings and set bacon aside. Add onions and sauté until translucent. Stir in cauliflower, broth and soup. Bring to a boil, reduce heat, cover and simmer 15 minutes or until cauliflower is soft. Add bacon and cheese. The cheese does not need to melt completely before blending.

At this point, you need to purée the mixture. You must be careful. Fill the blender about $1/3$-$1/2$ full, cover the lid with a dish towel to protect yourself from the hot liquid and purée in batches.

Return all soup to large pan and reheat gently. Taste for seasoning. Add salt and/or hot pepper sauce if desired.

8 cups

You can use the rind on the Brie because it does purée with the cauliflower mixture very well. If you use the spreadable Brie and feel you need a little more creamy texture, add 3 ounces cream cheese.

Inspiration: *Woman's Day*, 1998

Pear Brie Soup

3	cups chopped, fresh, ripe pears
3	cups chicken broth, divided
1/2	teaspoon cinnamon
1/2	teaspoon ground ginger
1/2	teaspoon ground cloves
1/4	cup butter or margarine
1/4	cup flour
1	cup heavy cream
8	ounces Brie cheese*, cut into 3-4 pieces
1-2	tablespoons fresh lemon juice

Heat pears, 2 cups chicken broth, cinnamon, ginger and cloves in a 2-quart or larger saucepan. Cook until pears are very tender (5-10 minutes). Purée in batches in a blender with a towel over the lid to prevent burns. (Don't wash your blender yet, we are going to use it again.)

In the same saucepan, melt butter. Add flour and cook over medium-low heat for about 1 minute. Add remaining 1 cup chicken broth and stir quickly to incorporate the flour mixture. Add pear mixture and heat to boiling, stirring constantly. Reduce heat and stir in cream. Put about 1 1/2 cups of soup back in the blender, add Brie and blend to combine. If the cheese is fresh and the rind is soft, use all the cheese – rind and all. If there are some hard spots on the rind, trim them off before blending.

Return cheese-pear mixture to saucepan and add lemon juice to taste. Start with 1 tablespoon, then taste – you just want to brighten up the taste, not overpower the soup.

6-7 servings

~

* Brie comes in many sizes so get close to the 8 ounces but don't buy extra to get exactly 8 ounces. The 5-ounce creme form is great for this soup because it has no rind. If you think you want more creamy texture, a couple ounces of cream cheese can be added.

~

Canned pears can be used. Buy the "Lite" variety to reduce sugar. Cook them 3-5 minutes to infuse the spice flavor.

~

Inspiration: *Pillsbury Classics No. 109*

Spinach Soup

This has a great surprise ingredient — white wine Worcestershire sauce.
Pictured on page 83.

Pictured on page 83.

5	tablespoons butter or margarine, divided
1	bunch green onions, sliced
½	(10-ounce) package fresh spinach, washed
3	cups chicken broth, divided
4	tablespoons flour
2-4	tablespoons white wine Worcestershire sauce
½	cup heavy cream

In a medium saucepan, melt 1 tablespoon butter or margarine. Add green onions and sauté until soft. Add spinach and 1 cup chicken broth. Cover and cook until spinach is wilted and tender (3-5 minutes). Put into blender or food processor; with a towel over the lid to prevent burns, blend until smooth.

In the same saucepan, melt remaining 4 tablespoons butter. Add flour and cook until bubbly. Add remaining chicken broth and spinach purée. Cook until it comes to a boil and soup thickens. Add Worcestershire sauce (start with 2 tablespoons and add more per your taste). Add cream and gently heat through. If you are making "Soup Under Wraps," chill soup and ladle into individual serving cups, then continue with recipe on opposite page.

4 cups

Inspiration: Lea & Perrins booklet when white wine Worcestershire sauce was introduced.

Tomato Soup

Pictured on page 83.

Pictured on page 83.

1	large onion, chopped
2	tablespoons butter or margarine
4	cloves garlic, chopped
1	(28-ounce) can crushed or diced tomatoes*
1½	cups water or tomato juice
½	teaspoon garlic salt (or to taste)
1	teaspoon rosemary
1	cup heavy cream
1-2	teaspoons fresh lemon juice, if needed

In a large saucepan, sauté onion with butter until soft and translucent. Add garlic and cook 1-2 minutes more, stirring constantly. Add remaining ingredients, except cream and lemon juice. Heat gently for about 10 minutes to blend flavors. If you want a very smooth soup and you used diced tomatoes, blend in small batches in a blender or food processor with a towel over the lid to prevent burns.

Add cream, stir and taste. If you used water you might want to add the lemon juice to zip the flavor up a bit. If you are serving this without a pastry crust, heat through and serve. If you are making "Soup Under Wraps," chill soup and ladle into individual serving cups, then continue with recipe on opposite page.

6 cups

* If you have great tasting fresh tomatoes, you can use them. It takes about 2 pounds. Cut them up and cook them with the onion, garlic and rosemary until very soft. Then blend and add cream.

Inspiration: *San Francisco Encore Cookbook*

Soup Under Wraps

Pictured on page 83.

General Directions

Puff Pastry: Each 17.3-ounce package of puff pastry has 2 sheets. You can get 4 pieces out of each sheet. Thaw the pastry sheets (overnight in the refrigerator works great). Unfold one thawed pastry sheet. With a rolling pin, lightly roll sheet to smooth out fold lines. Cut into 4 squares. Then cut the corners off each square to make a rough circle out of each piece.

Cooled soup of your choice (see Tomato Soup and Spinach Soup on opposite page) should be in serving bowls, no more than 4 inches in diameter. I've found that if the bowl is wider, the puff pastry tends to sink down into the soup before it can puff up (not good!).

Preheat oven to 400 degrees.

Place pastry circles over soup cups, press firmly around the edge and sides of the cup, brush with egg wash (1 egg mixed with 1 tablespoon water) and place on cookie sheet. Bake on the bottom rack of the oven for 20-25 minutes, until pastry is puffed and browned. Serve immediately. If you delay, they will hold 10 minutes or so. After that, they don't deflate, they just get cold.

This really makes a great presentation, but don't say bad things about me when you are washing the soup cups.

~

Inspiration: *The Pleasures of Cooking*

French Onion Soup

This is a simplified version of a great tasting soup.

3	large yellow onions, sliced thin
3	tablespoons butter
4	cups chicken broth
4	cups beef broth
1	tablespoon plus 1 teaspoon Maggi seasoning (or to taste)
2	cups dried bread cubes
4	ounces shredded mozzarella cheese (1 cup)

The first thing you need to do is find a saucepan that will hold the number of cups of soup you want to make. Fill the pan with water to the desired amount of soup, for our recipe, we need 8 cups. Notice the water level on the pan. Discard water.

In the saucepan over high heat, melt butter. Place sliced onions loosely in pan. They should be about even with the water line you marked in the beginning. Cover, reduce heat to medium and cook until onions are soft and translucent (5-8 minutes), stirring a couple times. Add chicken and beef broth. Bring to a boil then reduce heat and cook gently 30 minutes - 2 hours. The longer the better. During this cooking time, some of the broth will evaporate so keep adding water to maintain the 8 cup level. The longer the cooking time, the more the onions will break down and become easier to eat.

Just before serving, add Maggi seasoning (I use $1/2$ teaspoon per cup of soup). To serve, ladle into soup bowls, top with bread cubes and shredded cheese.

8 cups

~

This method: 1. measure the pan, 2. onions to the line, 3. broth to the line, 4. $1/2$ teaspoon Maggi seasoning per cup, works for small to large amounts of soup.

~

Inspiration: Suzie Timmons, a friend from Kansas City

Chicken Velvet Soup

Thanks, Nancy, for the book.

6	tablespoons butter or margarine
1/4	cup chopped onion
6	tablespoons flour
3	cups chicken broth
1	cup half and half or heavy cream
1	cup finely chopped cooked chicken
1/8-1/4	teaspoon garlic salt
1-2	teaspoons fresh lemon juice

Melt butter in a saucepan over medium-high heat. Add onion and sauté until translucent or soft, but not brown. Add flour and mix until all flour is combined. Cook about 30 seconds. Add chicken broth and heat to boiling, stirring constantly. Reduce heat and add cream, chicken, garlic salt and lemon juice. Heat through and taste for seasoning.

5 cups

~

This is a great winter soup when you have left over chicken. I use heavy cream because it makes a wonderful smoothness. It also will make the soup a little thicker, so add more broth if you like.

~

Inspiration: *I Could Eat Raw Dog* cookbook

Tomato Dill Soup

1/2	cup butter or margarine
1	cup finely chopped onion
1	cup finely chopped carrots
1	cup finely chopped celery
2-3	cloves garlic, minced
1/4-1/3	cup flour*
3	cups chicken broth
1	(28-ounce) can diced or crushed tomatoes (I use diced tomatoes for a chunky soup and crushed tomatoes for a smoother soup)
1	(15-ounce) can tomato sauce
1	cup heavy cream
1	teaspoon sugar
1	teaspoon dried dill weed or 1 tablespoon fresh dill (or to taste)

In a large saucepan over medium high heat, melt butter or margarine. Add onion, carrots and celery and cook until soft (4-6 minutes). Stir in garlic and heat just until you can smell the fragrance of the garlic. Stir in flour and cook 30 seconds to 1 minute to remove the starchy taste of the flour. Add chicken broth and bring to a boil. Add tomatoes and tomato sauce, reduce heat and simmer for 3-5 minutes.

Stir in cream and sugar and heat through. Check for salt. Just before serving, add dill.

*Use 1/4 cup flour if you use crushed tomatoes and use 1/3 cup flour if you use diced tomatoes.

8-9 cups

~

I love this soup because it uses canned tomatoes. In fact, unless you have your own fresh garden tomatoes, canned tomatoes in general have better flavor than fresh tomatoes from the market, for most cooked dishes. This soup freezes very well.

~

Inspiration: *Ladies' Home Journal*, 1996

Artichoke Cream Soup

This is rich and could be a great light supper dish on a cold night.

½	cup sliced green onions
½-¾	cup peeled & thinly sliced carrot circles*
½-¾	cup diced celery
8	ounces mushrooms, sliced
½	cup butter or margarine
½	cup flour
4	cups chicken broth
1	(14-ounce) can artichoke hearts, chopped, reserving juice
1	cup heavy cream
⅛-¼	teaspoon hot pepper sauce

In a large saucepan over medium-high heat, melt butter. Add onions, carrots, celery and mushrooms. Cook, stirring often, until vegetables are tender (5-10 minutes). Add flour and stir so vegetables are coated with flour. Continue to cook for about a minute — keep stirring. Add broth and reserved artichoke juice. Heat until liquid comes to a boil and mixture thickens. Reduce heat, add artichokes, cream and hot pepper sauce. Taste for seasoning. Heat through and serve.

*I love to use the mini carrots for this because they make such nice even, small circles. Slice carrots about ⅛-inch thick so they cook evenly with remaining vegetables.

Inspiration: *The Spirit of Christmas* book 2, 1988

Zucchini Bacon Soup

This is a great surprise soup — even for those who don't like zucchini!

4-6	cups coarsely chopped zucchini
3	cups beef broth
4	slices bacon, chopped
1	cup chopped onion
3	cloves garlic, minced
2	tablespoons butter or margarine
2	tablespoons flour
1	cup heavy cream

Heat zucchini, broth, bacon, onion and garlic in a large saucepan over high heat. If the broth doesn't cover the vegetables, add a little water. Bring to a boil then reduce heat and cook until zucchini is very soft (10-15 minutes). Purée in a blender (either allow the soup to cool before blending or blend in small batches with a towel over the lid to prevent burns).

In the same saucepan, melt butter. Add flour and cook until foamy (30 seconds - 1 minute). Add 1 cup cold water and bring to a boil. Add zucchini purée and bring back to a boil. Add cream and heat through. Taste for seasoning.

Large zucchini work fine in this soup, but cut in half and scrape the seeds out so the soup isn't too watery. The amount of butter and flour (roux) can be increased or decreased to desired consistency.

Inspiration: *Enjoy Make Ahead Dinner Party Menus* cookbook, 1989

Smoked Salmon-Filled Rigatoni

5-6 servings

~

Get the biggest diameter rigatoni you can find for easier filling. DeCecco is the brand I found best in our area.

~

You will use more cream and Romano cheese if you make these in individual dishes.

~

Inspiration: *McCalls*, 1988

30-35	rigatoni, plus a few extra for breakage
1	(8-ounce) tub of smoked salmon cream cheese
3	ounces smokey cheese, shredded (I've used Gouda and smokey cheddar. Both work fine.)
1/4	cup sliced green onions
1	tablespoon minced fresh dill, or 1/4 teaspoon dried dill weed
1	cup heavy cream, or more if necessary
1/2	cup grated Romano cheese
	chopped parsley

Cook rigatoni in salted water until al dente. Drain and cool.

Combine cream cheese, smokey cheese, green onions and dill.

Grease baking pan — the pan needed depends on how you are going to serve this dish. I serve this as an appetizer using 5-6 rigatoni per person baked in individual dishes. When baking all the pasta together, use a 7x11 or 9x13-inch baking pan. You want only <u>one layer</u> of pasta.

Preheat oven to 400 degrees.

Using a pastry tube with a 1/2-inch tip, fill each rigatoni and place in prepared pan. Pour cream around pasta until pasta is almost completely covered. Sprinkle with Romano cheese and bake 20-30 minutes, until cream is bubbly and cheese is browned.

To serve, sprinkle with a little chopped parsley.

Salmon Timbales with Cucumber Sauce

Sautéed cucumbers are the surprise in this recipe.

8 servings

Timbales

1	pound fresh salmon filet, skinned and cut in 1-inch cubes
4	eggs
1	teaspoon grated raw onion
3/4	teaspoon salt
3-4	drops hot pepper sauce
1 1/4	cups heavy cream, chilled (saving 1 tablespoon for sauce)

Sauce

1	tablespoon olive oil
1-2	small to medium cucumbers, peeled, halved lengthwise, seeded and sliced into 1/4-inch slices or chopped into 1/4-inch dice
2	tablespoons chopped shallots
1/4	cup white wine (I use vermouth)
1/4	cup white vinegar
1	tablespoon sour cream
1	cup butter, cut into tablespoons
1/2	teaspoon dried dill weed or 2 teaspoons fresh dill

Before food processors, dishes that had "puréed" meat or forcemeat were a real luxury because it was so labor intensive to push the meat through a mesh screen to get the smooth texture.

~

Inspiration: *The Pleasure of Cooking*

Preheat oven to 375 degrees. Grease 8 (4 or 5-ounce) ramekins or custard cups.

In a food processor, using the metal blade, coarsely chop salmon with 6-8 pulses. Add the eggs, onion, salt and hot pepper sauce. Process until smooth, about 1 minute, stopping once or twice to scrape down the bowl. With the machine running, pour cream through the feed tube in a thin, steady stream. When all the cream has been incorporated, scrape down the bowl and process 5 seconds more. Taste for seasoning.

Fill custard cups with 1/3 cup salmon mixture. Place cups in a 9x13-inch baking pan. Put hot water in the pan to come halfway up the sides of the cups. Cover with foil. Bake 15-20 minutes or until firm to the touch. Remove molds from water, run a small knife around the inside edge of each cup and unmold onto individual serving plates. Pour sauce (see below) over salmon or put sauce on plates first and salmon mold on top. Garnish with a little green such as parsley or a piece of fresh dill.

For Sauce: In a small frying pan, heat oil over medium-high heat. Add cucumbers and sauté until slightly soft, trying not to brown. Salt lightly and set aside.

In a small heavy-bottom saucepan over high heat, cook shallots, wine and vinegar. Boil until about 1 tablespoon of liquid remains. Add 1 tablespoon cream and sour cream then reduce heat to medium. Whisk in butter, one piece at a time, until all butter is incorporated. Add sautéed cucumbers and dill weed.

This recipe is for you, Amy Doerring!

Salmon Napoleons with Beurre Blanc

This is a wonderful first course. Even people that aren't salmon lovers like this. It is also a very economical way to serve fish in a menu. Pictured on page 83.

½ (17.3-ounce) package frozen puff pastry sheets (1 sheet)
1 pound salmon fillet

Preheat oven to 400 degrees.

Snap the sections of frozen puff pastry apart with a knife. Use the 2 largest sections. Save the third, smaller section for another time. Place the 2 pieces of puff pastry on a parchment-covered cookie sheet and bake on the bottom rack until puffed and golden (15-20 minutes). Remove from oven and cool slightly.

When cool enough to handle, cut the two strips of puff pastry in half, horizontally, so you have a top and bottom. You should now have four long pieces of puff pastry. Eventually you will be putting the halves back together, so position them on your baking sheet for easy reassembly (that is top up and bottom down).

Using a very sharp knife, cut very thin strips of salmon, placing them on the puff pastry until all four faces of puff pastry are covered with salmon.

Bake 5-8 minutes, until salmon is cooked and looks opaque. To serve, put the top portions of the salmon and puff pastry on the bottom portions. Cut each strip crosswise into four pieces and serve with beurre blanc.

Beurre Blanc

2 tablespoons chopped shallots
⅓ cup white wine (I use vermouth)
⅓ cup white vinegar
1 cup cold butter, cut in tablespoons

In a small, heavy-bottom saucepan, combine shallots, wine and vinegar. Boil until about 1 tablespoon of liquid remains. Reduce heat to medium and begin adding butter, 1 tablespoon at a time, whisking constantly until all butter is incorporated. Serve immediately.

The trick to this recipe is not to get it too hot when you add the butter. It will hold for a little while if you put it over simmering water.

Timbales of Crab & Spinach Mousse

This is an elegant first course. It can also be used as a luncheon entree if made in 6-ounce ramekins. Pictured on page 88.

8 first-course servings
or 6 luncheon entrees

~

Source:
Food & Wine, 1987

Spinach Mousse

2	tablespoons butter or margarine
2	tablespoons flour
1/2	cup heavy cream
3/4	cup half and half
1/4-1/2	teaspoon salt, to taste
1	(10-ounce) package frozen, chopped spinach, thawed and squeezed dry
3	eggs

Crabmeat Mixture

1	(6-ounce) can lump crabmeat, drained and cartiledge removed
2	eggs, well beaten
3	tablespoons heavy cream
1	teaspoon fresh lemon juice
	dash of hot pepper sauce
1/8	teaspoon celery salt
1/4	teaspoon garlic salt

Melt butter in a small saucepan. Add flour and cook about 30 seconds, until bubbly. Add 1/2 cup cream and half and half. Bring to boiling and cook about 1 minute. Remove from heat, season with salt. Add spinach and stir to combine. Place in bowl, cover with plastic wrap and cool completely. When cool, whisk eggs in, one at a time. Check for seasoning.

Preheat oven to 350 degrees. Grease 8 (4 or 5-ounce) custard cups or ramekins with butter or vegetable spray. A small piece of parchment paper in the bottom of the cup helps with unmolding, but it isn't life or death.

Distribute crab evenly into each cup. Combine remaining crabmeat mixture ingredients (eggs through garlic salt) and put about 2 tablespoons into each cup. Then add about 1/3 cup of the spinach mousse mixture to each cup.

Place cups in a baking pan and add hot water to halfway up the sides of the cups. Cover pan with foil and bake 30-40 minutes until mousse is set.

To serve, unmold timbales onto serving plates and top with *Beurre Blanc* (recipe on opposite page) or a light lemon sauce of your choice. If you are into garnishing, something red like a piece of red pepper or a tiny piece of parsley on top looks good.

Crab-Stuffed Mushrooms

This was one of the first items on our menu, and it still remains popular.

8 servings

Inspiration: This recipe is a combination of many recipes. I've found that butter sauce never hurts anything!

16	large button mushrooms (2-2$1/2$ inches in diameter)
8	ounces mushrooms, cleaned
2	tablespoons vegetable oil
1	(6-ounce) can crab, drained
1	teaspoon garlic salt
2	teaspoons fresh lemon juice
1	tablespoon chopped, ripe olives (4-5 large olives)
$1/3$	cup mayonnaise
5	tablespoons dry bread crumbs, divided

Preheat oven to 400 degrees.

To prepare the mushrooms for stuffing, remove stems (save for the stuffing) and, using a sharp knife, cut the shoulder of the mushroom down (save for stuffing) to make the cavity a little larger and easier to fill. Put prepared mushroom caps in greased 9x13-inch baking pan.

Chop the 8 ounces of mushrooms, stems and shoulders. In a medium skillet over medium-high heat, sauté mushroom pieces in vegetable oil until cooked and lightly brown. Transfer to a bowl and add crab, garlic salt, lemon juice, olives, mayonnaise, and 3 tablespoons of bread crumbs. Stir to combine. Taste for seasoning — you might want to add a little more lemon juice or salt, depending on the size of your mushrooms.

Divide mixture among the prepared mushrooms. Sprinkle remaining crumbs over the top, cover with foil and bake 20 minutes. Remove foil and continue to bake an additional 5-10 minutes, until tops are brown and mushrooms are cooked.

Serve with *Beurre Blanc Sauce* (page 12).

Four Cheese & Spinach Tart

The salami in this recipe gives it a special punch.

1	(9-inch) partially-baked, built-up tart or pie shell*
4	ounces provolone or mozzarella cheese, shredded (1 cup)
4	ounces Monterey Jack cheese, shredded (1 cup)
3	ounces cream cheese, softened
3	eggs
1/2	(10-ounce) package frozen, chopped spinach, thawed and squeezed dry (you can use the other 1/2 of the package for Ham & Chicken Manicotti or Chicken with Pastrami, Spinach & Cheese)
3/4	cup heavy cream
1/2	cup diced hard salami
3	tablespoons grated Romano cheese
	salt if necessary

Preheat oven to 325 degrees.

Combine all filling ingredients except salami and Romano cheese. Mix until blended. Add salami and stir. OR IF USING A FOOD PROCESSOR, put chunks of provolone and Jack cheese in with the metal blade and process. Then add cream cheese, eggs, spinach and cream and process again. Mix the salami in by hand.

Put filling into partially-baked crust and top with Romano cheese. Place on a cookie sheet and bake on the bottom rack of the oven 40-50 minutes, until puffed and brown. Let rest 5-10 minutes before serving. Garnish with slice of tomato.

8 servings

*I make a generous filling, so I always make a tart shell that is at least 1/4-inch above the rim.

Inspiration: *Better Homes & Gardens*, 1992

Onion Tart

I think people are afraid of this but it is sweet and wonderful.

1	prebaked 9-inch tart shell
2	large onions, thinly sliced (I use yellow onions)
2	tablespoons oil
3	slices of bacon, cut into julienne strips
4	eggs
3/4	cup heavy cream
1/2	teaspoon salt
1/2	teaspoon dried or 2 teaspoons fresh basil
1	large or 2 small Roma tomatoes — skin, ribs and seeds removed, flesh cut into julienne strips

In a medium frying pan, heat oil over medium heat. Add onion and stir to coat. Reduce heat to low, cover with waxed paper and cook 10-20 minutes, stirring frequently, until onions are completely cooked. They should not be brown.

While onions are cooking, fry bacon until brown, but not too crisp. Drain and set aside.

Preheat oven to 300 degrees.

In a mixing bowl or food processor, mix eggs, cream and salt (this can easily be mixed by hand with a whisk as well). Add basil — if you have fresh basil, it really makes a wonderful difference. I don't usually have fresh, so I use dried and it works fine. Taste for seasoning — remember there will be bacon but it still needs a little salt in the egg mixture.

Put cooked onions on the bottom of the baked tart shell. Sprinkle bacon and tomato over the onions then fill shell with egg mixture. Place on a cookie sheet and bake 45-55 minutes, until brown and set. Let rest about 10 minutes before serving.

---

8 first-course servings

~

I have a terrible time with this leaking as it bakes. That's why I put it on a cookie sheet. Try this trick — put about 1 cup of egg mixture on the onions, bacon and tomato and put it in the oven for about 10 minutes. If it leaks, the egg mixture will bake into the crust holes and then you will have a little seal on the crust. Then add the remainder of the filling.

~

Inspiration: *The Pleasures of Cooking*

Fried Pasta with Smoked Beef & Sun Dried Tomatoes

People are always surprised when you tell them they are having "fried" pasta. Pictured on page 81.

10-12 servings

These can be made ahead and refrigerated for several hours before cooking (covered lightly with paper towels or cloth).

Shells

20-24	large pasta shells, plus 5-10 extra for breakage
12	ounces cream cheese, softened
12	ounces Monterey Jack cheese, shredded (3 cups)
3-4	tablespoons chopped shallots (about 1 medium to large)
6	ounces oven-cured roast beef or smoked beef, chopped
8-10	sun dried tomato halves, packed in oil, chopped

Coating

2	eggs
1	tablespoon water
2	cups dried bread crumbs
1/3	cup Romano cheese
1/2	teaspoon Italian seasoning
1/2	teaspoon seasoned salt
1/4	teaspoon garlic salt
	flour to coat shells (about 1/2 cup)
	oil for deep frying

Cook shells in a large pan of salted water until al dente. Drain.

Combine cream cheese, Jack cheese, shallots, beef and tomatoes. Mix well. OR IF USING A FOOD PROCESSOR, with metal blade running, drop shallots into processor and chop. Add Jack cheese in 2-inch cubes and process. Add cream cheese and process again. Transfer mixture to a bowl and mix in tomatoes and beef.

In a small bowl, whisk together eggs and water. In a separate bowl, combine bread crumbs, Romano cheese, Italian seasoning, seasoned salt and garlic salt. Put flour in a third bowl.

Using about 2 tablespoons cheese mixture per shell, stuff cheese mixture into shell and wrap the shell around to enclose completely. Roll each filled shell in flour then egg mixture then bread crumbs. Place seam side down on a plate or countertop.

To cook, fill a deep saucepan no more than 1/3 full with oil. (I use vegetable or canola oil.) Heat to 360 degrees, using a thermometer to get an accurate temperature. Place a few shells at a time in the oil and cook until brown (about 1 minute). Drain on paper towels.

Sometimes, at this point, to be sure cheese is completely warm in the middle, I microwave them for 30-60 seconds, or until the cheese starts oozing out the ends of the shells. This is especially good if the shells have been chilled. You can also keep them warm in a low 200-degree oven if you are preparing large amounts.

Galettes of Dried Beef & Provolone with Fresh Spinach Sauce

9 servings
(I make 9 so that I can use the entire box of pastry.)

Inspiration:
Bon Appétit, 1984

I have converted more spinach haters to lovers with this recipe. Pictured on page 82.

Pastry

6	ounces oven-cured roast beef, at room temperature
8	ounces provolone cheese, at room temperature
1	(17.3-ounce) package frozen puff pastry sheets, thawed
1	egg, beaten with 1 tablespoon water for egg wash

Sauce

3	tablespoons chopped shallots (about 1 medium shallot)
1	tablespoon butter
2	tablespoons dry white wine, optional (I use vermouth)
2	cups lightly packed fresh spinach leaves (about $1/2$ of a 10-ounce package)
3	tablespoons butter
3	tablespoons flour
1	cup chicken broth
$3/4$	cup heavy cream

Preheat oven to 400 degrees.

In a food processor, combine beef and cheese and pulse until ingredients are chopped, or dice with a knife and combine in a bowl.

On a lightly floured surface, unfold one piece ($1/2$ of the total package) of the pastry. Lightly roll pastry with rolling pin until rectangle measures $10^1/2$ x $10^1/2$ inches. Cut out 9 circles, 3-$3^1/2$ inches in diameter. (I use my coffee pot lid. You'll just have to look around your kitchen for something 3-$3^1/2$ inches.) Repeat this step with the other piece ($1/2$) of pastry.

Place golf ball-sized balls of beef/cheese mixture on each of 9 pastry circles. (If the cheese is warm enough, the balls will hold their shape by squeezing tightly.) Place remaining pastry circles on top, stretch over the filling and seal the edges. This is the tricky part. I have tried everything to make a tight seal. The best success I've had is to press the edges very firmly all around then fold the edges toward the center and press again. I don't use any water or egg wash in the sealing process. I have never had 100 percent seals, but the stuffing can be pushed back in after it bakes and it works just fine.

Brush pastries with egg wash and bake 20-25 minutes in the lower third of the oven.

Sauce: In a small saucepan, sauté shallots in 1 tablespoon butter until soft. Add wine and cook 30 seconds or so to burn off alcohol. Add spinach and 1/2 cup water. Cover and cook until spinach wilts and is cooked (1-2 minutes). Put spinach mixture into a blender container and blend until smooth.

In same saucepan, melt 3 tablespoons butter, add flour and cook about one minute, stirring constantly. Add chicken broth and cook, stirring constantly, until mixture boils. Add puréed spinach and cream. Heat until warm. Check for seasoning. If it's too thick, add more cream or chicken broth. To serve, put about 1/4 cup sauce on a small plate and set pastry on top.

Salads
&
Dressings

Greens with Jack Cheese & Toasted Walnuts with Shallot Vinaigrette

6-8 servings

~

When I first made this dressing I liked the sugar in it, but as I get older I like things more tart so I now leave the sugar out.

~

If you have trouble shredding the cheese because it is too soft, place it in the freezer for $1/2$ hour or so to firm up before shredding.

~

Inspiration:
Bon Appétit, 1985

Salad

1-2	heads romaine lettuce (8-10 cups), cut, washed and drained
6	ounces Monterey Jack cheese, shredded ($1^{1}/2$ cups)
1	cup toasted walnuts, coarsely chopped

Dressing

2-3	large sprigs of parsley, just the tops
1	medium to large shallot
$1/3$	cup red wine vinegar
1	tablespoon Dijon mustard
$3/4$	teaspoon salt
	pepper to taste (I use $1/4$ teaspoon, but most people use more)
1	teaspoon sugar, optional
1	cup vegetable oil

Mix lettuce and cheese and place in refrigerator to keep cold.

In a small food processor with metal blade or in a blender container, put parsley, shallot, vinegar, mustard, salt, pepper and sugar, if desired. Blend until shallot is chopped. While processor is running, slowly add oil until dressing becomes thick.

Pour just enough dressing over greens and cheese to coat when tossed. (You will have more dressing than you need for one recipe. Just refrigerate it and use it again.) Add walnuts, toss lightly again and serve.

Hearts of Palm Salad

6 servings

Inspiration: *Bon Appétit*, 1987

Salad

1   large head romaine lettuce, chopped and washed

1   (14-ounce) can hearts of palm, drained and sliced into ½ inch slices

1   (14-ounce) can artichoke hearts, drained and coarsely chopped

½   pound bacon, diced, cooked until crisp and drained

½   cup diced, seeded tomato or 1 (2-ounce) jar chopped pimientos, drained

1   ounce blue cheese, slightly frozen

Dressing

¼   small onion

1   tablespoon deli-style mustard

1   teaspoon sugar, optional

1   teaspoon salt

⅛   teaspoon pepper

⅓   cup cider vinegar

1   cup vegetable oil

Combine all salad ingredients except blue cheese.

In a blender or food processor, combine onion, mustard, sugar, salt, pepper and vinegar. Blend or process to combine. With blender running, slowly add oil. Toss salad with only enough dressing to coat.

Grate blue cheese over salad and serve.

Semi-Caesar Salad

The "semi" means no egg. It can also mean mixed greens, no anchovies or no croutons. I love the freedom the word "semi" allows.

Salad

1	head romaine lettuce, cleaned and cut in bite-size pieces
$1/2$	cup Romano or Parmesan cheese
$1/2$-1	cup croutons*

Dressing

2	cloves garlic
1	teaspoon salt
3	anchovy fillets or 1 tablespoon anchovy paste
3	tablespoons sour cream
$1/2$	teaspoon pepper
$1/2$	cup red wine vinegar
$1^1/2$	cups vegetable oil

Put salad greens in large bowl. Mix all the dressing ingredients except oil in a blender container or food processor. While blender is running, slowly add oil.

When ready to serve, add cheese and croutons to greens. Toss salad with just enough dressing to coat lightly (you won't need it all).

*To make your own croutons, cut French bread or bread of your choice into cubes. Toss with melted butter and bake 8-10 minutes at 400 degrees. If I do it just right the outside is crispy and the center is still a little chewy. I get it right about 60% of the time.

4-6 servings

~

If you don't want to use the anchovies, it's still good, but give them a chance before you make up your mind. I used to always make this with 1 teaspoon garlic salt and I thought it was fine. Then one day I tried it with fresh garlic and I thought it was so much better. You can make up your own mind.

~

Inspiration: *San Francisco "a la carte"* cookbook

Romaine, Mandarin Orange & Glazed Almonds Salad

Salad

6-8	cups chopped greens, 1/2 romaine lettuce and 1/2 iceberg lettuce
3-4	green onions, sliced with some of the green tops
1	cup chopped celery
1	tablespoon butter
1/3	cup sugar
3/4	cup slivered almonds
1	teaspoon vanilla
	salt
1-2	(13-ounce) cans Mandarin oranges, drained

Dressing

2	tablespoons sugar
4	tablespoons white vinegar
1/2	teaspoon salt
1/8	teaspoon pepper
3-4	drops hot pepper sauce
3/4	cup vegetable oil

Salad: Combine greens, onions and celery in a bowl or plastic bag and refrigerate several hours to blend flavors.

Caramelized nuts: In a small skillet over medium heat, melt butter. Add sugar and almonds. Stir over medium heat until sugar melts and nuts are coated. It will be a creamy caramel color at this point. Remove from heat and add vanilla. When you add the vanilla, it turns a deeper brown color. Pour nuts out onto a sheet of aluminum foil or parchment paper, separating nuts as much as possible. Sprinkle with salt and continue to separate nuts until cool. Set aside.

Dressing: Combine sugar, vinegar, salt, pepper and hot sauce. Stir to dissolve sugar, add oil and shake or whisk vigorously.

To serve, combine greens, nuts and oranges. Toss with just enough dressing to coat lightly. Or place dressed greens on serving plates and top with oranges and almonds.

4-6 servings

Inspiration: my sister, Jan Mercer and Margaret Weston, a member of the first group to eat at our house.

Strawberry & Green Salad with Sweet Garlic Dressing

4-6 servings

Inspiration: Sargento advertisement 2000

This is a different strawberry salad with the garlic dressing and the addition of cheese.

Salad

6-8	cups mixed greens
2	cups sliced strawberries
½	cup toasted walnuts, chopped
1	cup shredded cheese — cojack or cheddar

Dressing

⅓	cup sugar
⅓	cup cider or red wine vinegar (I like cider best)
1	small clove garlic, minced
¼	teaspoon salt
¼	teaspoon paprika
⅛	teaspoon pepper
½	cup vegetable oil

For dressing: If you have a food processor, mix first six ingredients (sugar-pepper) and process to mince the garlic and dissolve the sugar. With the machine running, slowly add oil.

To make dressing without a processor, combine first six ingredients (sugar-pepper) in a bowl and whisk to dissolve sugar. Slowly add oil, whisking constantly.

In a large salad bowl, layer greens, strawberries, walnuts and cheese. Drizzle dressing over salad but don't toss. It's just too pretty to toss. If you want, you can toss the greens with a little dressing before you begin layering.

Greens & Strawberries with Poppy Seed Dressing

This is such a pretty salad and you'd be surprised how many like it.

Salad

4-6	cups greens — romaine, iceberg, butter lettuce, or a combination, cut into bite-size pieces
3	cups sliced fresh strawberries
1/2	cup thinly sliced or chopped sweet onion

Dressing

1/2	cup mayonnaise
1/4	cup sugar
2	tablespoons white vinegar
1/4	cup milk
1/4	teaspoon salt
1	teaspoon poppy seeds

Combine salad ingredients in a large bowl or divide among individual salad plates. For dressing, combine all ingredients and whisk briskly. Pour just enough dressing over salad to coat or drizzle over individual servings.

This recipe was in my file a long time — first from a friend, Helen Wolfmeyer, and then from the publication *Taste of Home*. I was a little hesitant to try the combination. Finally I did and we just love it. I go easy on the onion for myself but my husband loves the onion-strawberry thing.

Spinach & Vegetable Salad with Chutney Dressing

6-8 servings

~

I really like using iceberg or romaine with any spinach salad to give some body, so to speak, to the spinach. When the dressing is added to the salad, the spinach leaves stick together and the salad goes flat, if you don't have the lettuce mixed in with the spinach.

~

Inspiration for dressing: *Gourmet,* 1983

Salad

1	(10-ounce) package fresh spinach, cleaned & stems removed
1/2	head iceberg lettuce
2	cups chopped romaine lettuce
9-10	radishes, shredded (save some for garnish)
1	small head cauliflower, broken in bite-size pieces or sliced
1/2	cup shelled, salted sunflower seeds

Dressing

2	medium cloves garlic
1/2	cup red wine vinegar
1	tablespoon stone ground mustard
1/2	teaspoon salt
1/2	cup mango chutney
1	tablespoon sugar, or to taste
1 1/2	cups vegetable oil

Mix all salad ingredients together in a large bowl, except the radishes saved for garnish.

Combine all dressing ingredients except oil in a blender container or food processor. With machine running, slowly add oil.

Toss salad with dressing, using only enough to coat the greens. Top with reserved shredded radishes.

Spinach Bacon Salad

Salad

1	(10 ounce) bag fresh spinach, cleaned and stems removed
½	head romaine or iceberg lettuce
½	pound bacon, chopped, cooked until crisp and drained
1	(8-ounce) can sliced water chestnuts, chopped if desired
3	eggs, hard cooked and coarsely chopped
½	cup shelled, salted sunflower seeds

Dressing

¼	cup ketchup
¼	small onion
¼	cup red wine vinegar
2	tablespoons sugar
¼	teaspoon salt
¼	teaspoon pepper
¾	cup vegetable oil

I like to chop romaine before I wash it because there is a bitter liquid that is released when you cut it.

Chop and rinse romaine. Combine spinach and lettuce in a large bowl. Add remaining salad ingredients.

Combine all dressing ingredients except oil in a blender container or food processor. Blend to combine. With blender running, slowly add oil. Using only enough dressing to lightly coat, pour over lettuce and toss.

Broccoli, Bacon & Raisin Salad

6-8 servings

~

You can substitute dried cherries or dried cranberries (such as Craisins) for the raisins. You can also add small julienne strips of jicama for an additional crunch or 1 (11-ounce) can of Mandarin oranges, drained, for color.

~

Inspiration: *Iowa Farmer Today*, 1989

Salad

3-4	cups bite-size broccoli florets
2-3	cups bite-size cauliflower pieces
1/2	cup raisins
1/4	cup diced red onion or sweet onion such as Vidalia
1/2	pound bacon, chopped, cooked until crisp and drained
1/2-1	cup shelled, salted sunflower seeds

Dressing

3	tablespoons sugar
1/2	cup mayonnaise
1	tablespoon white vinegar

Put broccoli in microwave-safe bowl with 1 tablespoon water. Cover with plastic wrap and microwave 1-2 minutes until color brightens to a dark green. Drain and cool. Place all salad ingredients in a large bowl. Mix dressing ingredients and pour over salad. Toss to combine.

Cauliflower Bacon Salad

6 servings

~

Inspiration: This recipe comes from a very good friend, Judy Floss. I can still remember the dinner we had at their house when she served this salad. Great! I send this in my husband's lunch and it remains one of his favorites.

Salad

1	large head cauliflower, broken into bite-size pieces
1/2	pound bacon, chopped, cooked until crisp and drained
1/4	cup chopped red onion
1	cup shredded mozzarella cheese

Dressing

2	tablespoons bacon drippings (this is optional but adds great flavor)
1/4	cup sugar
1	cup salad dressing (I use Miracle Whip)
2	tablespoons white vinegar

Mix salad ingredients. Combine all dressing ingredients in a small bowl. Stir to dissolve sugar. Using as much dressing as you like, pour over salad ingredients and toss.

Hearts of Palm & Black Bean Salad

I just love this salad, so colorful and cool. Pictured on page 87.

6-8 servings

Salad

1	(15-16-ounce) can black beans, rinsed and drained
1	(11-ounce) can corn, drained
1	(16-ounce) can hearts of palm, drained and cut into 1/4-1/2 inch thick rounds
2	large tomatoes, seeded and diced (about 2 cups)
1/2	red onion, minced (about 1/2-3/4 cup)

Dressing

3	tablespoons fresh lime juice
1/2-3/4	teaspoon salt
1/2	teaspoon sugar
	pepper to taste
1	teaspoon coriander
1	teaspoon dried or 2 tablespoons minced fresh cilantro
1/4	cup vegetable oil

Mix all salad ingredients in a large bowl. In a separate small bowl, combine all dressing ingredients except oil (lime juice through cilantro). Stir to dissolve sugar and salt. Whisk oil into juice. Pour over salad and mix. Cover and refrigerate. This can be made one day ahead.

You can use 2 cans of corn if you need to make a little more salad with the same amount of dressing.

Inspiration:
Bon Appétit, 1987

Fresh Mushroom Salad

4-6 servings

~

Inspiration: *Gourmet,*
1975

Salad

4	cups sliced button mushrooms (very firm mushrooms work best)
1	cup diced celery
1/2	cup diced green pepper
1/2	cup diced red onion
1/2	cup diced red pepper or 1 small (2-ounce) jar chopped pimientos, drained

Dressing

1/3	cup red wine vinegar
1	teaspoon minced garlic
1	teaspoon Worcestershire sauce
1	teaspoon salt
1	cup olive or vegetable oil, or a combination

Mix all salad ingredients. Combine all dressing ingredients, except oil, in a bowl, stirring to dissolve salt. Whisking constantly, slowly add oil. Toss salad with just enough dressing to coat. Best to dress salad no more than 30 minutes before serving.

Red Cabbage Salad

Serves 6-8

~

* If you don't have chicken-flavoring from the noodle packet, use 1 teaspoon seasoned chicken base in the dressing.

~

Inspiration: This recipe was sent to me by Carol Oleson and it has become a favorite of our daughter Karlene.

This can also be made with broccoli slaw instead of cabbage.

Salad

1/2	medium head red cabbage, coarsely shredded
2-4	green onions, sliced
1/4	cup shelled, salted sunflower seeds
1	package chicken flavored Ramen noodles

Dressing

2	tablespoons sugar
3	tablespoons white vinegar
	seasoning from Ramen noodle packet*
1/3	cup vegetable oil

Combine cabbage, onion and sunflower seeds in a medium bowl. (The noodles go in the salad just before serving.) Before opening the noodle package, give it a couple whacks with a rolling pin or heavy pan to break the noodles into bite-size pieces. Remove the seasoning packet from the noodle package. Mix the sugar, vinegar and seasoning until sugar is dissolved. Then slowly add the oil, whisking constantly. Toss dressing with cabbage mixture. Just before serving, add noodles and mix again.

When I first read this recipe, I didn't know if the noodles were cooked before adding them to the salad. They are not! Just break them up and put in the salad right out of the package.

Sauerkraut Salad

1	(15-ounce) can sauerkraut
3/4	cup sugar
1	cup diced celery
1	cup diced green pepper
1/4	cup diced onion
3	tablespoons white vinegar
1/2	teaspoon salt
1/8	teaspoon pepper
1/8	teaspoon celery seed
2	(2-ounce) jars chopped pimiento, drained

Rinse and drain sauerkraut. Chop into 1-inch lengths and place in a large bowl. Add all remaining ingredients and mix well. Cover and refrigerate overnight. This keeps very well.

4-6 servings

This is a great novelty salad and has the bonus of no oil! You could even substitute a sugar alternative to make it very low in calories.

Wilted Cabbage Salad

Salad

1	medium head cabbage, shredded
1	small onion, chopped (about 1 cup)
1	green pepper, chopped (about 1 cup)
1	cup sliced pimiento-stuffed green olives

Dressing

1/2	cup sugar
1	teaspoon salt
1	cup white vinegar
1	teaspoon celery seed
1	teaspoon prepared mustard (I use deli-style or spicy brown)
1/8	teaspoon pepper
1/2	cup vegetable oil

Combine salad ingredients in a large bowl. Combine all dressing ingredients in a medium saucepan and bring to a boil. Boil three minutes, remove from heat and pour over salad ingredients. Refrigerate overnight. Keeps several days.

6-8 servings

Inspiration: My mother-in-law, Isabel Trusler

Pasta Salad with Mustard Dressing

8-10 servings

Inspiration: I know this was printed in *The Des Moines Register*, but I don't know the year.

Salad

2	cups uncooked pasta (i.e. rotini, twists)
1	(10-ounce) can artichoke hearts (quartered or whole), drained and coarsely chopped
1	medium green pepper, diced
1	medium red pepper, diced
20	baby carrots, thinly sliced into rounds
1/2	cup diced red onion
1	cup chopped celery

Dressing

1/2	cup vegetable oil
1/4	small onion
2	tablespoons grated Romano cheese
2	teaspoons salt
1/2	teaspoon dry mustard
1/2	teaspoon sugar
1/2	teaspoon dried or 2-3 leaves fresh basil
1/2	teaspoon pepper
1/4	cup red wine vinegar
1	tablespoon fresh lemon juice
1/4	cup Dijon mustard

Combine salad ingredients in a large bowl. Combine all dressing ingredients in a blender container and blend. Pour all dressing over salad. Cover and chill.

Dill Pasta Vegetable Salad

Salad
1½	cups uncooked pasta (i.e. elbow, shell, rotini)
½	cup sliced green onions
½	cup sliced pitted ripe olives
¼	cup sliced pimiento-stuffed green olives
¾	cup chopped red, green or yellow pepper, or a combination
1	cup tomatoes — sliced romas or halved cherry or grape tomatoes
4	ounces cheddar cheese, shredded (1 cup)

Dressing
¼	cup vegetable oil
2	tablespoons fresh lemon juice
2	tablespoons white wine vinegar
¾	teaspoon dried dill weed
¾	teaspoon dried oregano leaves
½	teaspoon salt

Cook pasta in salted water until desired doneness. (I like to cook pasta for cold salads a little longer than for baked casseroles.) Drain and rinse.

Combine all remaining salad ingredients except cheese. Combine dressing ingredients in a small bowl then pour over salad and mix. Add cheese and toss. Cover and chill.

6-8 servings

~

Purchased shredded cheddar cheese works well for this recipe because the shreds are larger than you can make at home and it holds its shape better in the salad.

~

Inspiration: *Southern Living,* 1991

Sweet Pasta Salad

1	pound pasta (rotini, rotelle, medium shells — your choice)
1	medium onion, finely chopped (about 1 cup)
2	cucumbers, seeded and finely chopped
1	green pepper, finely chopped
½	red pepper, finely chopped or 1 (4-ounce) jar chopped pimiento

Dressing
¾	cup white vinegar
¾	cup sugar
¾	cup vegetable oil
2	teaspoons salt
½	teaspoon pepper
2	teaspoons garlic powder
1	tablespoon dry mustard
3	tablespoons chopped parsley or 2 tablespoons dried parsley flakes

Cook pasta in salted water until done. Drain and put in a large bowl. Add vegetables.

For dressing, combine vinegar and sugar. Mix until sugar is dissolved. Add remaining dressing ingredients, pour over pasta and vegetables and toss to coat. Cover and chill 30 minutes, to blend flavors. Stays good for 1-2 days.

10-12 servings

~

Inspiration: This comes from a friend, JoAnn Ringger, who got it from another friend, Raylene Tisdale. JoAnn brought it to a salad luncheon and I just loved it for the sweet dressing and the finely chopped vegetables. We call it the JoAnn-Raylene salad, but that won't mean much to you!

Potato Salad

Potato salad is a very personal thing. Everyone has their own special touch. I've decided the best potato salad is the one your family will eat!

Serves 8

~

If you want to make the salad the day before, I like to cook the potatoes and add the onion and dressing. But cook and add the eggs the day of service otherwise they tend to get a little rubbery.

~

Inspiration: My mother-in-law, Isabel Trusler

Salad

1½	pounds potatoes, cooked and chopped, about 4 cups (I use red skin potatoes)*
4	eggs, cooked and chopped
½	small red onion, chopped (about ⅓ cup)

Dressing

1	cup Miracle Whip
¼	cup white or cider vinegar
¼	cup sugar
¼-½	teaspoon salt — start with ¼, taste and add more if needed
1	tablespoon deli-style mustard — or your choice
⅛	teaspoon pepper

Toss salad ingredients together. Combine all dressing ingredients and stir to blend. Pour over salad and stir to coat.

*I cook the potatoes in their skins until just done — try not to overcook the potatoes because it makes for a mushy salad. Peel the skins off as soon as the potatoes are cool enough to hold (it is just easier). Chop in desired size. I had orders (from my husband) to chop the potatoes into ¼-inch pieces because his mother did it that way.

Surprise Combination Salad

Great with a fish or chicken entrée. Pictured on page 88.

Salad

2	grapefruit
3	oranges
1	small onion, thinly sliced
2	cucumbers, seeded and sliced
1	apple, cored and cubed

Dressing

½	cup sugar
½	cup orange juice
½	cup red wine vinegar
¾	teaspoon salt
⅛	teaspoon pepper

To prepare grapefruit and oranges, slice skins off with a knife: Start by cutting off a slice on both ends of the fruit to make a flat surface. Place one end on the counter and, using a sharp knife, cut the skin and white membrane away from the outside of the fruit. To section, hold the peeled fruit in one hand and with a knife cut down one section line and then down the other to loosen each section and have no white membrane on fruit.

Combine grapefruit and orange slices with remaining salad ingredients. Combine all dressing ingredients, stirring to dissolve sugar. Pour over salad. Cover and chill 1-2 hours. At serving time, drain dressing and serve.

The ratio of fruits to vegetables is a personal choice. We prefer more oranges than grapefruit and more cucumbers than onion, but the combination really goes well together.

Inspiration: A recipe contest winner from the Florida Citrus Association, it was printed in *The Des Moines Register*, 1980

Creamy Cole Slaw Dressing

Sometimes you just want some plain old cole slaw and this dressing is the one I like the best, to date!

Makes about 3½ cups

Inspiration: *Bon Appétit*, 1976

2½	cups mayonnaise
½	cup cider vinegar
2	tablespoons plus 2 teaspoons prepared mustard (I use deli-style mustard)
1	tablespoon celery seed
¾	teaspoon pepper
1½	teaspoons salt
1	cup sugar
⅛	teaspoon paprika

Combine all ingredients and mix until smooth. Stores well in the refrigerator.

Strawberry Vinaigrette

This is good on mixed greens or spinach.

Makes 1¼ cups

~

Inspiration: *Creative Ideas*, 1987

1	green onion, cut in one-inch pieces
2	tablespoons light brown sugar
¼-½	teaspoon salt
¼	cup white vinegar
4-5	whole fresh or frozen strawberries, thawed
¾	cup vegetable oil

In blender or food processor combine all ingredients except oil. Blend or process mixture 10-15 seconds. With blender or processor running, add oil in a steady stream until all is incorporated.

Raspberry Vinaigrette

Makes about 2¾ cups

~

Inspiration: *Better Homes & Gardens*, 1988

¼	cup Raspberry Purée (page 130)
½	cup raspberry-flavored vinegar
¼	cup sugar
½	teaspoon salt
⅛	teaspoon cinnamon
2	cups vegetable oil

In bowl, blender or food processor combine all ingredients except oil. Whisk or blend mixture 10-15 seconds. With blender or processor running, add oil in a steady stream until all is incorporated. If you are using a whisk, pour oil in a little at a time whisking constantly.

This dressing is best drizzled on top of salad. If you toss the dressing with the salad, the color is not as pleasing.

Main Dish

Beef, Pork, Chicken, Casseroles

Beef Tenderloin with Mustard Balsamic Vinegar Sauce

4-6 servings,
1¼ cups sauce

~

Inspiration: *Good Housekeeping*, 1992

2	pounds beef tenderloin roast
1	medium shallot, minced (about 2 tablespoons)
2	tablespoons butter or margarine
2	tablespoons flour
½	cup beef broth
½	cup chicken broth
¼	cup balsamic vinegar
1	tablespoon Dijon mustard

Preheat oven to 475 degrees.

Salt beef and bake 25-30 minutes. Roasts usually have a thinner end and a thicker end, so in 25-30 minutes you can get a medium well on the thinner end and more medium to medium rare on the thicker end. If you have an instant read thermometer, use it. The medium well should be about 145 degrees and the medium rare should be about 135 degrees. Remove from oven and let rest at least 10 minutes.

Sauce: Melt butter in a small saucepan. Add shallots and sauté until soft (about 1 minute). Add flour and cook until foamy. Add beef and chicken broth and bring to a boil. Stir in vinegar and mustard.

Beef with Wine Sauce

This is great, and maybe even better made the day before and reheated. Pictured on page 89.

6-10 servings

3-4	pounds boneless beef (I use short ribs, boneless top blade chuck steak or boneless chuck roast)
1/2	teaspoon leaf thyme, or to taste
4	tablespoons vegetable oil, divided
1 1/2	cups chopped carrots
1 1/2	cups chopped celery
1 1/2	cups chopped onion
1/2	cup chopped shallots
2-3	cloves garlic, chopped
6	tablespoons balsamic vinegar
1	cup red wine (cabernet, merlot or your choice)
1	cup beef broth (or one 10^3/4-ounce can beef broth)

Season meat with salt, pepper and thyme.

In a large skillet, heat 2 tablespoons oil over medium heat. Add meat and brown on both sides. Put in an oven-proof roasting pan that has a lid or can be covered with foil.

Using the same skillet, heat 2 tablespoons oil. Add carrots, celery, onion and shallots and sauté until vegetables are slightly soft. Add chopped garlic and sauté 1-2 minutes more to bring out the oils in the garlic. Add vinegar, wine and broth and pour over meat. Cover tightly and bake in 300 degree oven until very tender. This can take 2-3 hours for blade steak, up to 8 hours for short ribs. Just check it to see how tender you like it. There is no need to preheat the oven for this dish.

Sauce: Remove meat from pan and keep warm, leaving vegetables and liquid. Put liquid and vegetables in small batches in a blender container. With a towel over the lid to prevent burns, blend until smooth. This is the sauce; however when you blend, air gets incorporated and the color is not good. So put it in a saucepan and bring to a boil to remove some of the air. The darker color will return. If the sauce is too thin, thicken it with a slurry of equal parts cornstarch and water, bringing it back to a boil one more time.

Serve sauce over meat or on the side.

You could add sautéed mushrooms to the sauce and cut the meat into bite-size pieces and serve it over noodles. Great buffet dish.

Five Hour Stew

This is more like a pot roast than a stew.

2	cups tomato juice
3	tablespoons pearl barley or 3 tablespoons pearl-size tapioca
2	teaspoons seasoned salt
2	tablespoons Worcestershire sauce
2	pounds lean beef stew meat, cubed (1-2-inch pieces) chuck roast or 7 blade roast
2	cups carrots, cut into 1-inch pieces, (you can also use whole baby carrots)
3	cups potatoes, cut into 1-inch pieces
1½	cups celery, cut into 1-inch pieces
2	large onions, quartered

Preheat oven to 275 degrees.

Combine tomato juice, barley, salt and Worcestershire sauce and let soak while you cut up the vegetables. Combine meat and vegetables in a large, covered casserole dish or Dutch oven. Pour juice over meat and vegetables and mix lightly. Cover tightly and bake 5 hours stirring a couple times during baking.

6 servings

If you would like to leave the house while this is cooking, cut a piece of waxed paper or parchment paper the size of your pan and place it directly onto the meat and vegetables. This will help prevent burns to the top layer.

Inspiration: *Wallaces Farmer Magazine,* 1970

Stove Top Casserole

I think every family has a dish that is called "the old standby." This is ours. It's one of those recipes you usually have the ingredients for, takes little time to prepare and everyone will eat it.

1	pound ground beef
½	medium onion, chopped
1	cup uncooked elbow macaroni
1	(15-ounce) can mixed vegetables, undrained
1	(10¾-ounce) can tomato soup
½	cup water
1	cup shredded cabbage
1½	teaspoons seasoned salt

In a medium skillet over medium high heat, brown ground beef and onion. Drain off excess fat, if needed. Add remaining ingredients to ground beef mixture in skillet. Stir and cover. Reduce heat to medium and cook until macaroni is done, about 10 minutes, stirring frequently to prevent sticking.

4-6 servings

This dish is very versatile. You can use whatever vegetable you like, tomato sauce or picante sauce or a combination of sauces. The trick is to add enough liquid to cook the pasta. I added the cabbage to bulk up the vegetable servings, but if you don't like cabbage, you can easily leave it out. You may need to add some more water to get the macaroni cooked. Different brands of macaroni have different thicknesses.

Cheesy Taco Casserole

A great way to combine macaroni and cheese and taco salad.

8-10 servings

Inspiration: *Iowa Farmer Today*, 1987

2	cups uncooked macaroni
1/2	cup milk
6	ounces (1 1/2 cups) Velveeta, cubed
2	pounds lean ground beef
1	medium onion, chopped (about 1 cup)
1/4	teaspoon salt
1	packet taco seasoning or more to taste
1	(15-ounce) can chili beans or kidney beans, optional
2	(15-ounce) cans tomato sauce
2	cups shredded lettuce
2	medium tomatoes, seeded and chopped (about 2 cups)
4	ounces shredded cheddar cheese (1 cup)

Cook macaroni in salted water just until done. Drain and return to saucepan. Add milk and Velveeta cubes. Stir over low heat until cheese melts. Pour into a greased 9x13-inch baking dish. Set aside.

Preheat oven to 375 degrees.

In a sauté pan, cook ground beef and onion until beef is brown and onions are translucent. Sprinkle with salt and drain, if necessary. Return to pan and add taco seasoning, beans and tomato sauce. Stir to combine and pour over macaroni in baking dish. Cover with foil and bake 20-25 minutes, until heated through. You can also cover with foil and refrigerate overnight, then heat the next day (add 5-10 minutes to baking time). To serve, top with lettuce, tomatoes and cheddar cheese.

Tex-Italian Pasta Fiesta

This won a prize in a picante sauce contest!

8-10 servings

* If you use a 9x13-inch baking dish, the layers will be very thin. If you use a smaller dish, such as a 2-quart casserole, the layers will be thicker and therefore the cooking time will be slightly longer.

Inspiration: *The Des Moines Register*, 1996. The spinach layer idea was also used in a *Better Homes & Gardens* recipe in 1976.

8	ounces dry pasta (about 2 cups), I like smaller pasta (i.e. elbow or small shell pasta) in casseroles, but use your choice
1	(10-ounce) package frozen chopped spinach, thawed & squeezed dry
8	ounces cream cheese, softened
1/2	cup milk
1	teaspoon dried leaf oregano
1 1/2	pounds lean ground beef
1/4	teaspoon salt
2	cloves garlic, minced
1	(15-ounce) can tomato sauce
2	cups picante sauce, mild or medium
2	teaspoons chili powder
1 1/2	teaspoons ground cumin
6	ounces (1 1/2 cups) shredded mozzarella or cheddar cheese
	ripe olives and green onion slices for garnish, optional

Cook pasta in salted water until just done. Drain and rinse. Combine spinach, cream cheese, milk and oregano. Mix well.

Preheat oven to 350 degrees.

In a large saucepan or Dutch oven, brown ground beef and sprinkle with salt. Add garlic and cook until the fragrant oils are released. Drain if necessary. Return to pan and add tomato sauce, picante sauce, chili powder and cumin. Bring to a boil, reduce heat and simmer, uncovered, for five minutes. Add pasta and mix well. Spoon half of the pasta mixture into a lightly greased 9x13-inch baking dish*. Top evenly with spinach mixture and then the remaining pasta mixture. Cover loosely with foil and bake 30-40 minutes. Uncover and sprinkle with cheese. Bake 2 more minutes to melt cheese. Top as desired with garnish.

Marinated Pork Tenderloin Medallions

This also makes a great sandwich using cocktail-size buns.

½	cup olive or vegetable oil
3	tablespoons white wine vinegar
½	small onion
2	cloves garlic
½	teaspoon salt
½	teaspoon chili powder
½	teaspoon dried leaf oregano
4	pork tenderloins (3-4 pounds total weight)

Combine first seven ingredients (oil through oregano) in a blender or food processor. Blend until onion and garlic are finely chopped. Put tenderloins in a large plastic bag and pour marinade over meat. Seal bag and refrigerate at least 8 hours or overnight, turning occasionally.

Preheat oven to 425 degrees.

Place tenderloins in shallow roasting pan. Put as much marinade as possible on top of the meat, then put the remaining in the pan. Bake 25-35 minutes, until internal temperature reaches 155 degrees. Remove from oven and let rest 10-15 minutes. Serve warm or at room temperature. Great with Ginger Mayonnaise (recipe below).

10-12 servings

Also great on the grill.

Inspiration: *Southern Living*, 1991

Ginger Mayonnaise

2	cups mayonnaise
1½	tablespoons white wine vinegar
2	tablespoons minced chives
½	teaspoon ground ginger
¼	teaspoon salt

Combine all ingredients, cover and chill.

Inspiration: *Southern Living*, 1991

Pork Tenderloin Tournedos

Putting the bacon inside and rolling it up makes a pretty presentation. Pictured on page 90.

Pictured on page 90.

One tenderloin serves 2-3 people

~

The picture on page 90 shows a little pink in the center of the meat. That is the way I like it and it is perfectly safe. But if that is not the way you like it, cook an additional 5-10 minutes, depending on the size of the tenderloins.

~

Inspiration: this idea came from preparing flank steak with this method.

   pork tenderloin (I use $1/2$ pound per person, but that is very generous)
1 pound bacon (for eight people), cut in 2-inch julienne strips, fried crisp and drained (see "ramblings," page vii for cutting technique) garlic powder
1 cup heavy cream for sauce

Preheat oven to 425 degrees.

Open the tenderloin for stuffing by laying it on the counter with the widest (or flattest) part on top. With a long, sharp knife, cut down the center almost to the bottom, but not through. Open the meat. Then with your knife flat, or parallel with the counter, carefully cut each half again, starting your second and third cuts where the first cut stopped, not cutting through. Open each half so the meat is completely flat on the counter. If the tenderloin is very big, you may have to cut each side one more time. Lightly pound the cuts to even out the meat. Sprinkle with a little garlic powder. Distribute cooked bacon over the meat using about $1/4$ cup per tenderloin. Then, as tightly as possible, roll the tenderloin up, jelly roll fashion, starting on the long side, pressing firmly to seal the edge. Place seam side down on a greased baking pan.

Bake 25-30 minutes, until browned and internal temperature is 155 degrees. Remove from oven and let rest 5-10 minutes. Slice and serve with cream sauce if desired.

Cream Sauce: This is a reduction sauce so you can use either a heavy large saucepan or a skillet for faster reduction. Boil cream until reduced by about half. Add any drippings from your meat, scraping any brown bits that are in the pan. Continue reducing until desired thickness. (An alternative to the reduction method is to heat the cream and juices and add a slurry of equal parts cornstarch and water until you get the desired consistency.)

Sauces for Pork Tenderloin

Orange Currant Sauce

1	tablespoon butter
1	small shallot, minced (1-2 tablespoons)
1	cup chicken broth
1/2	cup currant jelly
2	tablespoons orange juice concentrate
1	tablespoon cornstarch mixed with 1 tablespoon water

Melt butter in a small saucepan. Add shallots and sauté until soft (about 1 minute). Add broth, jelly and orange juice concentrate. Stir to dissolve jelly. Slowly add the cornstarch mixture until you get the desired thickness when mixture comes to a boil.

Makes 1 1/2 cups

Inspiration: *The Pleasures of Cooking* cookbook, 1985

Cream Sauce & Cream Sauce with Mustard

There is no trick to making a good sauce if you use meat juices and heavy cream. That's what I use.

After you cook the meat, if there are any brown bits in the cooking pan, scrape them up along with any juices that have collected. If you don't have enough juices, add a little broth – either chicken or beef and chicken combined. Put all this into a saucepan and add 1 cup heavy cream. To thicken, you can reduce the liquid or use equal parts cornstarch and water – adding just enough to the boiling liquid to get the right thickness.

To make the mustard sauce, I use natural stone-ground mustard to give a texture to the sauce. Start with 1 tablespoon then add more if you like the flavor.

Chutney Cream

2	tablespoons butter or margarine
1	medium shallot, chopped (about 3 tablespoons)
1/2	cup mango chutney
1	cup heavy cream
1/2	cup chicken broth plus any juices from pork
1	tablespoon cornstarch plus 1 tablespoon water

Makes 2 cups

Inspiration: *Sunset,* 1989

In a small saucepan, melt butter. Add shallots and sauté about one minute to soften. Add chutney, cream, broth and meat juices. Cook briefly, until heated through. If you want a completely smooth sauce, put mixture in a blender container and blend until smooth. Return the blended sauce to pan and thicken to desired consistency by gradually adding the cornstarch mixture (it must come to a boil for maximum thickening). If you like the chunky pieces, just heat and thicken as above.

Cornish Hen with Sausage & Mushroom Stuffing

4 servings

Inspiration: This is a combination of many recipes I've read.

This is very impressive if you serve a whole hen per person, but a very big serving. If the hens are very big, half per person is really plenty. Pictured on page 82.

| 4 | (20-ounce) Cornish hens, thawed (they all say 20 ounces, but some are bigger) |

Stuffing – for 4 boned hens, you will only use 3/4 of this for bone-in hens

8	ounces French bread, cubed
6	ounces pork sausage (I use 1/2 regular-flavored and 1/2 sage-flavored)
2	tablespoons butter or margarine
1	small to medium onion, chopped (about 1 cup)
1	cup chopped celery
4	ounces fresh mushrooms, chopped
3	ounces California dried apricots, chopped
1-2	teaspoons poultry seasoning (this is a personal choice and also depends on the sausage you use)
1-1 1/2	cups chicken broth
4	(6-inch) bamboo skewers

Glaze

1/2	cup currant jelly
1/4	cup chili sauce
1	tablespoon fresh lemon juice
1/8	teaspoon ground ginger

At our house, we serve the hens with the chest, back and thigh boned out. If you don't want to do this, ask your butcher. (I taught my butcher how to do this! That was fun. I learned from pictures in a magazine.)

Place bread cubes in a large bowl. If you have time, let the bread dry out a bit, because they will absorb more chicken broth and have more flavor.

Brown the sausage in a medium sauté pan over high heat, breaking it up into small pieces. Drain, if necessary, and add to bread cubes. In the same pan, melt butter. Add onion, celery and mushrooms and sauté until onions are translucent and mushrooms are cooked. Add this mixture to bread cubes. Add apricots and poultry seasoning. Then start adding chicken broth. Add about one cup and toss to distribute. Wait a couple minutes so that the bread has a chance to absorb the broth. Continue adding broth until bread is moistened through but not soggy. You'll know how you like your dressing after you make it once or twice.

Preheat oven to 400 degrees.

To stuff a boned hen – lay the hen skin side down, and salt lightly. Place about 1 cup of dressing in the center, on top of the breast meat. Bring the two sides up and over the dressing and secure using a 6-inch bamboo skewer. Place seam side down on a greased or parchment-covered pan. Repeat with remaining hens.

To stuff a bone-in hen – lightly salt the cavity and place 1/2-3/4 cup stuffing inside. Don't pack because it will expand some. Place hen on a greased or parchment-covered pan.

Bake 40-50 minutes for a boned hen, 50-60 minutes for a bone-in hen, until golden brown. About 5 minutes before hens are done, brush glaze over the tops. Be sure to get the drumstick covered because that is the best part!

Glaze: In a small saucepan over high heat, mix all glaze ingredients and cook until thick and syrupy, about five minutes, stirring frequently.

Seafood Casserole

This recipe started as a crab dip recipe from two dear friends – Dorothy Forsythe and Lou Ankeny. I just loved the flavor so I tried to make a casserole and it worked pretty well.

6-8 servings

6	tablespoons butter or margarine
2	bunches green onions, sliced using some of the green (1-1½ cups total)
3	large ribs celery, chopped (1-1½ cups)
1	(10¾-ounce) can cream of shrimp soup
1	(10¾-ounce) can cream of celery soup
8	ounces cream cheese
1	cup half and half
2	tablespoons fresh lemon juice
¼-½	teaspoon garlic powder
2	cups cooked rice (¾ cup uncooked rice)
2	(12-ounce) packages surimi crab, lobster or shrimp, or a combination, cut in bite size pieces
1	can sliced water chestnuts, chopped
2	cups fresh bread crumbs (2-3 slices)
2	tablespoons butter or margarine, melted

Preheat oven to 375 degrees.

In a large skillet or saucepan over medium-high heat, melt butter. Add green onion and celery and sauté until onions are tender and celery is crisp-tender (3-4 minutes).

Add soups, cream cheese and half & half. Heat until smooth. Add lemon juice and garlic powder. Taste for seasoning.

In a greased 9x13-inch casserole dish, layer rice, fish & water chestnuts. Cover with sauce mixture. Gently move fish and rice with a spoon to let sauce get to the bottom of the dish. Combine crumbs and butter and sprinkle over casserole. Cover with foil. Bake 30 minutes or until bubbly. Remove foil and bake 5-10 minutes more to brown the top.

You can use fresh or canned seafood if you like it better and can afford the cost.

This can be made the day ahead. Just bring it to room temperature and bake as directed or bake directly from the refrigerator adding 10-15 minutes to the cooking time.

Gâteau Florentine

This is a layered luncheon entrée that looks complicated, but it just takes some time and can be done the day before. Pictured on page 88.

Pictured on page 88.

6-8 servings

The picture on page 88 shows the gâteau with chicken.

* Salting is tricky because the salt in the cheese varies. Keep tasting the fillings after you add the cheese sauce or cheese to be sure you don't over salt.

Some of my customers like this with a little chicken in the layers. I use 3 cooked chicken breast halves, chopped fine and sprinkled over the mushroom filling. The picture on page 88 shows the gâteau with chicken. The chicken provides a little more height to the dish which makes a better picture!

Inspiration: *Bon Appétit*, 1981

Crepes – *This recipe is enough for 10-12 crepes. You only need 8 for the recipe, but you'll probably have some that don't turn out.*

1½	cups milk
1	cup flour
3	eggs
¼	teaspoon salt

Cheese Sauce

4	tablespoons butter or margarine
4	tablespoons flour
1½	cups milk
6	ounces Monterey Jack cheese, shredded

Spinach Filling

1	tablespoon vegetable oil
½	cup sliced green onions
1	(10-ounce) package frozen, chopped spinach, thawed and squeezed dry
2	teaspoons fresh lemon juice
¼	teaspoon salt*

Mushroom Filling

2	tablespoons vegetable oil
8	ounces mushrooms, cleaned and chopped
½	cup sliced green onions
8	ounces cream cheese, softened
1	egg
2	ounces (½ cup) Monterey Jack cheese, shredded
	salt to taste
¼	cup grated Romano cheese

Crepes: Combine ingredients in order in a blender container. Blend until smooth, scraping down the sides once or twice. Let rest 30 minutes.

Heat a non-stick skillet over high heat–the diameter of the bottom of the skillet should be the diameter of the crepe (9 inches). Brush with a thin layer of vegetable oil and pour about ¼ cup of the batter in the skillet. Tilt the pan to spread the batter around. Sometimes I spread the batter up the sides of the pan to get the diameter I need for my crepe.

Cook until bubbles form on top (15-20 seconds). Turn over (if you are brave you can flip it, but I use my fingers) and continue to cook another 10 seconds or so until very lightly brown. Turn out onto a tea towel. Repeat with remaining batter.

I have been known to piece these crepes together to fill in holes and/or make the right size for my pan, so don't worry.

Cheese Sauce: Melt butter in a medium saucepan over medium-high heat. Add flour and cook until bubbly. Add milk and cook until thick, stirring constantly. Add cheese, stir and set aside.

Spinach Filling: Heat vegetable oil in a medium sauté pan. Add green onions and sauté for about 1 minute to soften. Remove from heat and add spinach, lemon juice, salt and half of the cheese sauce. Stir to blend.

Mushroom Filling: Heat oil in medium skillet over medium-high heat. Add mushrooms and onions and sauté until mushrooms are cooked and beginning to brown. Remove from heat.

In a medium bowl, beat cream cheese & egg until smooth. Stir in cheese and mushrooms and stir to blend. Season with salt to taste.

To Assemble: Preheat oven to 400 degrees. In a greased 9-inch springform pan or any 9-inch pan with at least 2-inch sides, place one crepe in the bottom. Spread $1/4$ of the spinach filling. Top with second crepe and spread with $1/3$ of the mushroom filling. Repeat layering–you will have 4 layers of spinach and 3 layers of mushrooms. Then put one more crepe on top. Cover with remaining cheese sauce and sprinkle with Romano cheese.

Bake 25-30 minutes until brown and bubbly. Let rest 5-10 minutes for easier slicing.

Stuffed Chicken Breast Basics

Everyone has a favorite stuffed chicken recipe, and why not! It's a great way to serve chicken. You can pound it thin, spread it with a savory spread, roll it up like a jelly roll, bake it and slice. You can pound it thin and wrap it around packets of a variety of fillings. You can even cut pockets in the chicken breast and stuff it–this way it retains the shape of the chicken.

If you boned the chicken breast yourself, you will have a large section and a smaller section called the tender on the underside or closest to the bone. You can use this or you can save it for another time. The tender has a long tendon that should be removed before you use it. If you purchased boneless, skinless chicken breasts, they probably won't have the tender.

Sometimes at the large end of the breast, there is a tough section of gristle or tendon or something. I cut this out before continuing.

If you want to flatten a breast for filling:
1. *Start with a large breast half (6-8 oz.).*
2. *Lay the skinned side down on a work surface.*
3. *Place plastic wrap on the breast.*
4. *Using a flat pounder, pound from the center out to the edge until it is evenly ¼-inch thick.*
5. *Gently pound the edges a little bit thinner to help with the rolling and sealing later.*
6. *Place filling almost in the center of the flattened chicken.*
7. *Bring one section of chicken over the top of the filling, then fold in sides and roll over the remaining chicken.*
8. *Coat as desired.*
9. *Chill before cooking for best results.*
10. *Top with a pat of margarine or spray with vegetable spray to help in browning.*

I don't like to use toothpicks to secure the filling unless I have to because it is such a nuisance to get them out before you serve. If you place the rolled breast seam side down on the baking sheet, it should hold well enough.

The coating process is the classic 3-step process: First flour, then egg wash then crumbs of your choice.

I usually season the chicken itself not the flour. It takes about 1 cup to easily coat 6-8 breasts. Throw away any unused flour or you can use it to thicken any sauce for the chicken.

The egg wash for 6-8 servings is 2 eggs plus 2 tablespoons water. Mix thoroughly to break up the egg.

The crumb mixture gives the crunch that you want. You can use dry bread crumbs, fresh bread crumbs, cracker crumbs, corn flake crumbs, dry potato flakes or Japanese bread crumbs called "Panko" just to name a few. I usually take the easy way and use purchased dry bread crumbs but I have used all the others and they do have their own good qualities. I season the crumbs using such things as seasoned salt, garlic salt or dry herbs such as Italian mix, basil, oregano, dill, pepper, etc. You decide. My idea is to go easy on the seasoning because you are trying to taste the chicken rather than the coating. 1½-2 cups crumbs will coat 6-8 breasts, except for fresh bread crumbs – which will take more.

To help give a brown appearance when baked, add paprika to the crumb mixture and put a small pat of margarine on top of each coated chicken prior to baking. A light coating of vegetable spray works too. I found that butter just foams up and doesn't work as well as margarine.

The last thing is baking. I like to bake them in a hot oven (400-425 degrees) for a short time (20-25 minutes) rather than 350 degrees for 30-40 minutes. For me, I like the color and the chicken doesn't overcook as easily.

There is a new wrinkle in purchasing chicken and, for that matter, other packaged meats. Some processors are injecting flavor enhancers into the meat which is basically a salt solution. When using these meats, it's not necessary to add additional salt.

Good luck. Practice helps!

Chicken Fromage

For Each Serving

1	large boneless, skinless, chicken breast half, flattened
1	strip Muenster cheese (1"x 1½"x ¼")
1	strip Monterey Jack cheese (1"x 1½"x ¼")
1	strip chilled butter (1"x 1½"x ¼")
1	pat of margarine

Coating – for 6-8 breasts

1	cup flour
2	eggs
2	tablespoons water
1½	cups dry bread crumbs
½	teaspoon seasoned salt
½	teaspoon garlic salt

Inspiration: the classic Chicken Kiev recipe

Preheat oven to 400 degrees.

Lay flattened chicken breast on counter skinned side down. Place one piece of cheese near the center of the breast, place butter on top and then top with remaining piece of cheese.

Gently wrap the chicken around the cheese. This looks more like a box than a roll because the cheese is in a rectangular shape.

In a small bowl, combine eggs and water. In another bowl, combine bread crumbs, seasoned salt and garlic salt. Roll each chicken in flour then egg mixture then crumb mixture. Place on a greased or parchment-covered baking sheet and put a small pat of margarine on top or spray with vegetable spray. Chill if you have time. Bake 20-25 minutes. If you see cheese oozing out, the chicken is done.

Chicken with Herb & Garlic Cheese

Inspiration: this is a variation of the puff pastry recipe from *Southern Living,* 1991

For Each Serving

1	large boneless, skinless chicken breast half, flattened (instructions on page 50)
	sprinkle of garlic powder
1	tablespoon chive and onion flavored cream cheese
1	pat margarine

Coating – for 6-8 breasts

1	cup flour
2	eggs
2	tablespoons water
1½	cups dry bread crumbs
½	teaspoon garlic salt
½	teaspoon seasoned salt
¼	teaspoon Italian seasoning

Preheat oven to 400 degrees.

Lay flattened chicken breast on counter, skinned side down, and sprinkle with a little garlic powder. Place cream cheese in the center and wrap the chicken around the cheese as tightly as you can so cheese is completely covered. In a small bowl, combine eggs and water. In another bowl, combine bread crumbs, garlic salt, seasoned salt and Italian seasoning. Roll each chicken in flour then egg mixture then crumb mixture. Place on a greased or parchment-covered baking sheet and put a small pat of margarine on top or spray with vegetable spray. Chill if you have time. Bake at 400 degrees for 20-25 minutes.

Chicken with Pastrami, Spinach & Cheese

Pictured on page 86.

Inspiration: *Bon Appétit* Favorite Restaurant Recipes

For Each Serving

1   large boneless, skinless chicken breast, flattened (instructions on page 50)

1 or 2   thin slices pastrami or meat of your choice (I like the spice of the pastrami)

1   cube of Monterey Jack cheese (1-inch)

1   tablespoon of spinach mixture (see below)

1   pat of margarine

Spinach Mixture – for 6-8 breasts

$\frac{1}{2}$ (10-ounce) package frozen, chopped spinach, thawed and squeezed dry (sorry about using just $\frac{1}{2}$ a package, you can use the other $\frac{1}{2}$ for the Four Cheese & Spinach Tart, page 15 or Ham & Chicken Cannelloni, page 63)

1   egg yolk

$\frac{1}{4}$ cup grated Romano cheese

Coating

1   cup flour

2   eggs

2   tablespoons water

$1\frac{1}{2}$ cups dry bread crumbs

$\frac{1}{2}$ teaspoon garlic salt

$\frac{1}{2}$ teaspoon seasoned salt

$\frac{1}{4}$ teaspoon Italian seasoning

Preheat oven to 400 degrees.

Combine all spinach mixture ingredients. Lay flattened chicken on counter, skinned side down. Place one or two slices of pastrami on chicken then spread spinach mixture over the top. Place a cube of cheese on top of the spinach mixture. Fold the pastrami and spinach around the cheese, then turn over so the seam is against the chicken breast. Now wrap the chicken around the pastrami packet, sealing as best you can. (Turning the pastrami packet over helps the cheese stay in a little better.)

In a small bowl, combine eggs and water. In another bowl, combine bread crumbs, garlic salt, seasoned salt and Italian seasoning. Roll each chicken in flour then egg mixture then crumb mixture and place on a greased or parchment-covered baking sheet. Top each chicken with a pat of margarine or spray with vegetable spray. Bake 20-25 minutes.

Spinach-Stuffed Chicken

The spinach mixture in this dish rolls up with the chicken rather than just being a filling inside. Pictured on page 86.

Chicken
6-8	boneless, skinless chicken breasts, flattened instructions on page 50)
8	ounces cream cheese, softened
1	(1-ounce) envelope dry onion soup mix
1	(10-ounce) package frozen chopped spinach, thawed and squeezed dry

Coating for hot
1	cup flour
2	eggs
2	tablespoons water
1½	cups dry bread crumbs
½	teaspoon seasoned salt
¼	teaspoon paprika

Coating for cold
2-3	tablespoons fresh lemon juice
	paprika

Preheat oven to 400 degrees.

Thoroughly mix together cream cheese, soup mix and spinach. Lay flattened chicken breast skinned side down on the counter and spread spinach mixture over chicken, leaving about ½-inch edge on all sides.

Starting at one end, tightly roll the chicken into a cylinder – jelly roll fashion. Finish with either of the following options:

1. **If you plan to serve this as a hot entrée**, in a small bowl, combine eggs and water. In another bowl, combine bread crumbs, seasoned salt and paprika. Roll each chicken in flour then egg mixture then crumb mixture. Place on a greased or parchment-covered baking sheet and put a small pat of margarine on top or spray with vegetable spray. Bake 20-25 minutes, until brown.

2. **If you would like to serve this cold**, either as an hors d'oeuvre or a snack with crackers, place uncoated chicken rolls on a greased baking sheet. Brush with 2-3 tablespoons lemon juice and sprinkle with paprika. Bake 20-25 minutes until firm to the touch and pink color is gone. The trick is not to overbake. Remove from oven and chill. When ready to serve, thinly slice and serve with crackers.

6-8 main dish servings or 40-45 slices

Inspiration: I think this is from the onion soup package, but I don't have any documentation. In fact, I didn't actually have a recipe until now.

Chicken with Sun Dried Tomatoes & Mushrooms

6	large boneless, skinless chicken breast halves
8	ounces mushrooms, chopped
1	medium shallot, chopped
6-10	sun dried tomato halves, packed in oil, chopped (start with 6, then if you like the flavor, add more)
6	1½ x ½ x ¼-inch sticks of Monterey Jack cheese
1	cup flour
2	eggs
2	tablespoons water
1½	cups dry bread crumbs
½	teaspoon garlic salt, or to taste
	oil for browning (these days, I'm using canola oil)

6 servings

Inspiration: *Cooking Light,* 1997

To prepare chicken breast, remove all visible fat and tendons or gristle. Place skinned side <u>up</u> on the counter. With a long, thin-bladed knife, make a pocket in the thick end of the breast, trying to stay as close to the top of the breast as possible. Enlarge the cavity by moving the tip of the knife from side to side to make the pocket bigger, but keeping the opening just big enough to stuff. Repeat with remaining breast halves and set aside.

In a medium frying pan, heat 1 tablespoon of oil. Add mushrooms and shallots, cook and stir until mushrooms are brown and have lost most of their moisture. Remove from heat and add tomatoes. Cool.

To stuff the chicken, put 1-2 teaspoons mushroom mixture in the cavity, then push in the cheese stick and more mushroom mixture. If you didn't cut a deep enough cavity, just cut off the cheese to fit. Close the opening using a toothpick.

In a small bowl, combine eggs and water. In another bowl, combine bread crumbs and garlic salt. Roll each chicken in flour then egg mixture then crumbs. (Japanese style crumbs called "Panko" are really good for this recipe.)

Preheat oven to 425 degrees.

In a large sauté pan over medium-high heat, add oil to about ¼-inch depth. When oil is hot, put chicken breast in, skinned side down. Brown 3-5 minutes per side, place on baking sheet and bake 10-15 minutes, or until firm to the touch.

I usually serve this without a sauce because I use the Panko crumbs. If you use regular bread crumbs, a sauce is fine. If you would like a sauce, this is what I would use:

1-2	tablespoons chopped shallots or green onions
2	tablespoons butter
2	tablespoons white wine (I use Vermouth)
1	cup chicken broth
1	teaspoon cornstarch
1	teaspoon water

In a small saucepan, sauté shallots in butter until translucent. Add wine and reduce until most of the wine is gone. Add chicken broth and cornstarch mixed with water and bring to a boil to thicken.

Crab-Stuffed Chicken Breasts

6 servings

~

Inspiration: *Bon Appétit*, 1992

6	large boneless, skinless chicken breast halves
6	ounces cream cheese, softened
1	large shallot, chopped
1	(6-ounce) can crab, drained
1-2	teaspoons fresh lemon juice
1/4	teaspoon garlic salt
1	cup flour
2	eggs
2	tablespoons water
1 1/2	cups dry bread crumbs
1/2	teaspoon garlic salt, or to taste
	oil for browning (these days, I'm using canola oil)

To prepare chicken breasts, remove all visible fat and any tough tendon or gristle. Place skinned side up on the counter. With a long, thin-bladed knife, make a pocket in the thick end of the breast, trying to stay as close to the top of the breast as possible. Enlarge the cavity by moving the tip of the knife from side to side to make the pocket bigger, but keeping the opening just big enough to stuff. Repeat with remaining breast halves and set aside.

Combine cream cheese, shallots, crab, lemon juice to taste and garlic salt. Stuff mixture into the pocket of each chicken breast and seal with a toothpick. In a small bowl, combine eggs and water. In another bowl, combine bread crumbs and garlic salt. Roll each chicken in flour then egg mixture then crumbs. (I've used the Japanese-style bread crumbs called "Panko" for this and it is really good but regular dried bread crumbs are fine.)

Preheat oven to 425 degrees.

Heat a large sauté pan over high heat. Add oil to about 1/4-inch depth. When oil is hot, add chicken breasts, skinned side down. Turn heat down to medium high and brown (3-5 minutes) on each side. Place breasts on a baking sheet and put in the oven for 10-15 minutes, until firm and cooked through.

Chicken with Raspberry Vinegar Sauce

If you like color and fruit flavor with chicken, this is a winner!

6 servings

Inspiration: *365 Ways
to Cook Chicken*

6	boneless, skinless chicken breast halves
	salt
	flour to lightly coat chicken
	oil for frying

Sauce

½	cup raspberry-flavored vinegar
1	cup chicken broth
3	tablespoons Raspberry Purée (page 130)
1	cup heavy cream

If the chicken breasts are very thick at one end, pound slightly to make an even thickness. Season with salt and coat with a very thin layer of flour. The instant blend flour (Wondra brand) works good for this.

Preheat oven to 400 degrees.

Heat about ¼-inch depth of oil in a frying pan over medium-high heat. You can do this in one large pan or two batches in a smaller pan, but you should use fresh oil for each batch to get the best browning. The oil should be quite hot. Starting with skinned side down, sauté chicken until nice and brown on both sides. This take 3-4 minutes per side. Place chicken on baking sheet and put in the oven to finish cooking and stay hot (5-10 minutes).

Sauce: Discard oil in the pan, saving any brown bits that are on the bottom of the pan. Over medium-high heat, deglaze the pan with the raspberry vinegar, scraping the bottom to get all the flavor bits. Continue cooking until vinegar is reduced by about half. Add chicken broth, raspberry purée and cream. Continue cooking until sauce is reduced to desired thickness. If you are in a hurry, you can thicken the sauce with a slurry of equal parts water and cornstarch.

Remove chicken from oven, place on a serving platter, and coat with raspberry sauce or pass sauce separately.

Chicken in Phyllo with Cream Sauce

8 servings

~

Inspiration: A friend,
Charlotte Smith, gave
me a recipe similar to
this to make for her.

8	large boneless, skinless chicken breast halves
1/2	cup butter or margarine
1/2	cup flour
2	cups chicken broth
1	cup heavy cream
2	tablespoons coarse-ground mustard
1	(16-ounce) package phyllo dough, thawed
1/2-1	cup butter or margarine, melted

Trim any fat or gristle from chicken breasts. In a medium saucepan, melt 1/2 cup butter. Add flour and cook until foamy, stirring constantly. Add chicken broth, cream and mustard. Heat until thick and bubbly. Remove from heat, cover surface with plastic wrap to prevent a film from forming and cool completely. (I am usually in a hurry so I put this sauce on a baking sheet to cool quickly.)

When ready to wrap chicken, unfold the phyllo dough and lay flat on the counter. Place one sheet on a work surface with the long side toward you and brush with melted butter (not every inch needs to be covered with butter). Place a second sheet of phyllo on top of the first and brush with melted butter. Repeat with two more layers, for a total of 4 sheets. Cover remaining phyllo with a cloth to prevent drying.

Preheat oven to 425 degrees.

Cut the dough in half, top to bottom. You now have one rectangle on your left and one on your right. Place one chicken breast on each half about 3 inches from the bottom edge. Salt lightly. Place about 3 tablespoons of cooled sauce on top of chicken.

Bring the 3-inch piece up and over the top of the chicken, roll chicken once, fold the sides in toward chicken and roll one more time to make a rectangular packet. Place on a greased (or parchment-covered) baking sheet and brush top with butter. Repeat folding process for remaining chicken. Bake 20-25 minutes, or until brown. (When the phyllo is brown, the chicken is done.)

You should have some sauce left. Reheat to make a sauce to use after the chicken is done. You might have to add some liquid (water or cream) to make the right consistency.

Chicken in Phyllo with Lemon & Green Onion Sauce

This is the same idea as the phyllo with cream sauce.

8 servings

~

Inspiration: *Southern Living*

8	large boneless, skinless chicken breast halves
2	cups mayonnaise
1	cup sliced green onions
3	tablespoons fresh lemon juice
¼	teaspoon garlic powder
1	teaspoon chicken base
	heavy cream

Preheat oven to 425 degrees.

Mix all sauce ingredients (mayonnaise through garlic powder) and proceed wrapping the chicken as in *Chicken with Cream Sauce* (opposite page). Bake 20-25 minutes until packets are lightly brown.

Put remaining sauce into a saucepan, add 1 teaspoon chicken base and heat, whisking to combine. Add a little cream to get the desired consistency.

Chicken in Puff Pastry

This is a very impressive presentation for a chicken dish. The recipe is for seven only because you will use 1 complete box of puff pastry. Pictured on page 87.

Pictured on page 87.

1	(17.3-ounce) box puff pastry sheets
7	boneless, skinless chicken breast halves
	garlic powder
6	ounces chive and onion flavored cream cheese
1	egg, plus 1 tablespoon water

Thaw puff pastry. I like to put it in the refrigerator overnight. It also works if you leave it on the counter in the box for 1-2 hours. If you need it in a hurry, remove the two sheets from the package and let them thaw individually on the counter. It's best to wrap them with plastic wrap so they don't dry out. This takes about 30 minutes.

When pastry is thawed, unfold each sheet. Gently roll with a rolling pin to an 11x11-inch square. Cut each pastry sheet into quarters. You will use seven quarters to wrap the chicken and one quarter for decoration.

Preheat oven to 425 degrees.

Lay one chicken breast, skinned side down, on each puff pastry quarter. Sprinkle with a little salt and garlic powder (go easy) and place about a tablespoon of cream cheese in the middle of the chicken. Fold chicken over cheese then turn the chicken over so that the seam is touching the puff pastry. Bring opposite corners of the puff pastry together over the chicken and pinch to seal. Repeat with the remaining two corners of puff pastry. Seal edges well. Turn over and place on a greased or parchment-covered baking sheet.

For decoration, cut the remaining quarter of puff pastry into 14 strips. Using two strips per chicken bundle, twist one strip at a time and put around the bundle like a package. Seal ends of the strips on the bottom of the bundle.

Brush each chicken packet with egg wash mixture and bake on the bottom rack of oven 25-30 minutes, until pastry is puffed and golden brown.

7 servings

Note that this recipe does not require flattening the chicken breast.

Inspiration: *Southern Living*, 1991

Fiesta Chicken & Fiesta Chicken Casserole

1	cup cheddar cheese cracker crumbs
2	tablespoons taco seasoning mix
8	boneless, skinless chicken breast halves
1	bunch green onions, sliced using some of the green (about 3/4 cup)
2	tablespoons butter or margarine
2	cups heavy cream
1/2-1	(4-ounce) can chopped green chilies
1	teaspoon chicken-flavored soup base
4	ounces shredded Monterey Jack cheese (1 cup)
4	ounces shredded cheddar cheese (1 cup)

Preheat oven to 400 degrees.

Combine cracker crumbs and taco seasoning in a small bowl. Dredge chicken breasts in crumb mixture and place in a greased 9x13-inch baking dish.

In a medium microwave-safe bowl, microwave the butter or margarine and green onions for 2 minutes or until onions are soft (or sauté onions in a fry pan with butter). Add cream, chilies and soup base and stir. Pour cream mixture over chicken. Top with shredded cheeses and bake, uncovered for 25 minutes, until cheese is brown. To serve, gently cut around each breast with a sharp knife to cut the cheese so that the first serving doesn't pull all the cheese off the remaining chicken.

Fiesta Chicken Casserole is the same as above with these simple adjustments: reduce chicken to five or six chicken breast halves (2-3 lbs.) and add the following ingredients:

3	cups cooked rice (about 1 1/3 cups uncooked)
2	medium tomatoes, seeded and chopped
1/2	cup sliced ripe olives

Cut chicken breasts into 1-inch pieces and dredge in crumbs and seasoning, as directed above. In a 9x13-inch greased baking dish, layer cooked rice, tomatoes, olives and chicken. Pour sauce over chicken, sprinkle cheese on top and bake as above.

8 servings

~

This makes the best sauce so have lots of rice.

~

Inspiration: *Southern Living*

Chicken Casserole

10-12 servings

If you have any crescent rolls left over (page 70) they make wonderful pre-buttered crumbs!

Inspiration: When I started catering I knew I needed a basic chicken casserole, so I combined several recipes and came up with this basic one.

This is a basic casserole – I use more chicken than noodles, but use what you have.

8	ounces egg noodles
4	cups chopped, cooked chicken (I use both dark and white meat)
1	(8-ounce) can sliced water chestnuts, drained & chopped
1	(4-ounce) can mushrooms, sliced or pieces, drained
6	ounces cubed or shredded cheese (I use cubes of Velveeta or shredded American)

Sauce

1/4	cup margarine
1	cup chopped celery
1	cup chopped onion
1	(10½-ounce) can cream of celery soup
1	(10½-ounce) can chicken broth
½	cup mayonnaise
1	cup heavy cream
2	tablespoons fresh lemon juice
½	cup bread crumbs
1	teaspoon butter or margarine, melted

Cook noodles in salted water just until al dente. (Don't overcook because they will cook more during baking.) Drain and place in a greased 9x13-inch baking dish. Top with layers of chicken, water chestnuts, mushrooms and cheese. (I like layering the casserole because I want everyone to get some chicken in their serving, not just noodles.)

Preheat oven to 400 degrees.

Sauce: In a large saucepan, melt margarine. Add celery and onion and sauté until onions are translucent. Add soup, broth, mayonnaise and cream. Heat to combine. Add lemon juice and gently pour over casserole, moving the ingredients with a spoon so the sauce gets distributed throughout the casserole. Combine bread crumbs and margarine and sprinkle over the top of casserole. Cover with foil, place on a baking sheet to catch any spills and bake 40-45 minutes. (If made ahead and refrigerated, increase baking time to 1 hour.) The last 5-10 minutes of baking time remove foil and let crumbs brown. Let rest 10-15 minutes before serving.

Ham & Chicken Cannelloni

When filled with cheese, these pasta shells are called manicotti. When filled with meat, they are called cannelloni.

8	manicotti (cannelloni) pasta shells

Sauce

¼	cup butter or margarine
1	clove garlic, minced
¼	cup flour
2	cups half and half
1	teaspoon chicken-flavored soup base or bouillon granules
½	cup grated Romano cheese
⅛	teaspoon white pepper

Filling

¼	cup sliced green onions
2	tablespoons butter or margarine
½	(10-ounce) package frozen, chopped spinach, thawed and squeezed dry*
1	cup (about ⅓ pound) chopped cooked chicken
1	cup (about ⅓ pound) chopped cooked ham (use your food processor for these if you have one)
¼	cup grated Romano cheese
2	eggs, beaten
1	teaspoon fresh lemon juice
2	tablespoons grated Romano cheese for garnish, optional

Cook cannelloni in boiling salted water until al dente. Drain.

While pasta is cooking, make the sauce. Melt butter in a medium saucepan. Add garlic and cook 30 seconds to release the oils. Add flour and cook until bubbly (about 30 seconds). Add half and half and soup base and bring to a boil to thicken. Remove from heat, add cheese and white pepper. Keep warm.

Preheat oven to 350 degrees.

Filling: The green onions need to be cooked slightly in the butter. Do this in the microwave for about 1½ minutes or use a frying pan on the stove.

In a large bowl, combine onions and the remaining filling ingredients except Romano cheese, with about ⅓ of the cheese sauce. (This is just an "about" measurement – don't dirty another cup trying to get it exact!) Mix well. Using your fingers, stuff shells and place in a 7x11-inch greased casserole dish. Cover with remaining sauce (you may need to thin the sauce with a little half and half or water if it is too thick) and sprinkle with Romano cheese, if desired. Bake, covered, for about 20 minutes then uncover and bake until lightly brown and bubbly (10 minutes or so).

4-6 servings

~

* Four Cheese & Spinach Tart (page 15) or Chicken with Pastrami, Spinach and Cheese (page 53) also use ½ package of spinach.

~

This is easy to make ahead and heat up for use. Just remember it will take 10-15 minutes longer to bake.

~

Inspiration: I didn't document this recipe and I've looked through all my cookbooks, but be assured it didn't come to me in a dream!

Ham & Chicken Bake with Artichokes

I like ham and chicken together, so this recipe caught my eye.

8-10 servings

~

If you can find artichoke heart quarters, they are less expensive and work great for this recipe.

~

Inspiration: *Fanfair Cookbook*, 1990

8	ounces pasta (wide noodles, rotini or elbow)
2	cups cubed cooked ham
2	cups cubed cooked chicken
1	(13-14-ounce) can artichoke hearts, drained – reserving liquid, and coarsely chopped
4	tablespoons butter or margarine
1	medium onion, chopped (about 1 cup)
$1/2$	medium green pepper, diced (about $1/2$ cup)
$1/2$	medium red pepper, diced (about $1/2$ cup)
4	tablespoons flour
1	cup chicken broth
1	cup milk
1	($10^3/4$-ounce) can condensed cream of celery soup
1	cup sour cream
2	tablespoons butter, melted
1	cup dry bread crumbs
1	cup shredded cheddar cheese

Cook pasta in salted water. Drain and put in a 9x13-inch baking dish. Spread ham, chicken and artichokes over pasta.

Preheat oven to 400 degrees.

Melt butter in a large saucepan. Add onion, green and red pepper and cook until vegetables are tender. Add flour and cook 30 seconds more. Add chicken broth and milk. Bring to a boil and cook about 1 minute. Add celery soup, sour cream and juice from the artichokes. Heat and stir to blend soup. Do not boil. Taste sauce for salt. (There is a lot of salt in the chicken broth, artichoke juice and ham, so it's better not to over salt.)

Pour sauce over casserole using a spoon to move the noodles to distribute the sauce. Combine melted butter and bread crumbs and sprinkle around the edges of the casserole. Sprinkle cheddar cheese in the middle. Cover with foil and bake 35-45 minutes, until hot and bubbly. Remove foil for the last 5 minutes to brown.

Creamy Pasta with Ham & Broccoli

A quick, easy on-top-of-the-stove supper dish.

4-6 servings

8	ounces pasta (rotini, rotelle or medium pasta shells)
1	tablespoon butter or margarine
2	tablespoons vegetable oil
8	ounces mushrooms, sliced
2	cloves garlic, minced
2	cups cubed, cooked ham
1/2-1	(10-ounce) package chopped broccoli, thawed & drained (if you like broccoli, use the whole package, if you are trying to sneak green vegetables into your diet, use half the package)
1	cup heavy cream
1/4	cup grated Romano cheese

Cook pasta in boiling, salted water until al dente. Drain & set aside.

While pasta is cooking, make the sauce. Melt butter in a large sauté pan. Add oil and mushrooms and sauté until mushrooms are brown. Add garlic, cook and stir 30 seconds. Add ham, broccoli, cream and cheese and cook to thicken sauce slightly. Add pasta, toss and heat through.

Inspiration: This is from a combination of things I had in my refrigerator and reading many pasta recipes.

Ham, Broccoli & Rice Casserole

6 servings

~

Bread crumbs could be sprinkled on top for a garnish.

~

Inspiration: *Wallace Farmer*, 1975

1	cup uncooked rice (I use converted rice)
2	cups water
1/2	teaspoon salt
2	cups fresh broccoli (or 1 10-ounce bag of frozen broccoli pieces, thawed)
1/4	cup butter or margarine
1/4	cup flour
2	cups milk
2	tablespoons fresh lemon juice
1/4	teaspoon salt
1	cup sour cream
2	cups cooked ham, cubed
4	ounces shredded cheddar cheese (1 cup)

Cook rice in 2 cups water with 1/2 teaspoon salt until done (about 25 minutes).

If using fresh broccoli, peel stems and chop stems and florets into bite-size pieces. Cook in boiling, salted water just until bright green and crisp-tender (2-3 minutes). Drain.

Preheat oven to 400 degrees. Grease a 9x13-inch baking dish.

Melt butter in a saucepan over medium heat. Add flour and stir until mixture cooks and looks a little foamy (30-60 seconds). Add milk and bring to a boil, stirring constantly. Remove from heat, stir in lemon juice, salt and sour cream.

Pour about 1/2 cup of sauce into prepared baking dish. Layer rice, broccoli and ham in dish and pour the remainder of the sauce over the top, moving layers slightly to allow sauce to get to the bottom. Top with cheddar cheese, cover with aluminum foil and bake 20-25 minutes, until bubbly. Remove foil and bake another 5 minutes, to brown. Remove from oven and let rest 5-10 minutes before serving.

Egg Casserole

Cheese Sauce

4	tablespoons butter
4	tablespoons flour
1/2	teaspoon salt
2	cups milk
6	ounces American or Velveeta cheese (1 1/2 cups)

Bread crumbs

3	slices bread
1	tablespoon butter, melted
1/4	teaspoon paprika

Casserole

4	tablespoons butter
1/2	cup sliced green onions
18	eggs, beaten
1	(4-ounce) can mushroom pieces (if you like mushrooms, use 2 cans)
1 1/2	cups cooked ham, diced or 1 pound bacon, chopped and cooked crisp

Sauce: In a medium saucepan, melt butter. Add flour and salt. Cook and stir until bubbly (about 30 seconds). Add milk and bring to a boil. Remove from heat, add cheese and stir to melt. Set aside and keep warm.

Bread Crumbs: Break each bread slice into 2-3 pieces and put in a blender or food processor. Remove from blender, add melted butter and paprika. Mix well.

Preheat oven to 350 degrees.

Casserole: In a large frying pan, melt butter. Add green onions and sauté until softened. Add eggs and scramble just until set and still moist. Take off the heat and add mushrooms and ham. Fold in cheese sauce and pour into a greased 9x13-inch baking dish. Top with bread crumbs and bake 30-40 minutes.

If you don't have a large enough pan, divide the butter and eggs in half and scramble in two batches.

10-12 servings

This can be made the night before, covered and refrigerated to bake the next day (remove cover for baking). Add 10-15 minutes to baking time.

Inspiration: *Better Homes & Gardens,* 1976

B.O.O.M. Quiche

The B.O.O.M. stands for bacon, onions, olives and mushrooms.

8 servings	

Notice there is no added salt in this recipe. That is not an omission.

Inspiration: *San Diego Home & Garden,* 1984

1	partially baked 10-inch pie crust (instructions on page 116), try to get a nice high edge because the filling comes very close to the top
6-8	slices bacon, chopped in small dice or julienne strips
6-8	ounces mushrooms, sliced (if you really like mushrooms, go ahead and use the whole 8 oz. package)
8	ounces Monterey Jack cheese, shredded (2 cups)
8	ounces mozzarella cheese, shredded (2 cups)
1/3	cup sliced black olives
1/3	cup sliced green onions
2	tablespoons flour
4	eggs, beaten
1 1/4	cups milk
4	ounces cheddar cheese, shredded (1 cup)

Preheat oven to 350 degrees.

Fry bacon until crisp. Drain, reserving 1 tablespoon of fat, set bacon aside. Sauté mushrooms in reserved fat until lightly brown.

In the cooled pie shell, add Monterey Jack and mozzarella cheeses. Sprinkle bacon, mushrooms, green onions and olives over the cheese. Gently mix the cheese and vegetables. Combine flour, eggs and milk. Whisk and pour over cheese mixture. Top with cheddar cheese. Bake on the bottom rack of the oven 50-60 minutes until puffed and brown. Let stand 10-15 minutes before serving.

It is difficult to check this dish for doneness because the melted cheese sticks to the knife when you try to test it. Just take it out when puffed and brown and let it rest and it will be fine.

Bread, Pasta

&

Rice

Crescent Rolls & Cinnamon Twist Danish

These are the lightest rolls I've ever made. Pictured on the cover and page 84.

1	cup warm water (105-110 degrees)
3	tablespoons yeast (or 3 packages)
1	tablespoon sugar
2	cups liquid (milk, water or half of each)
1	cup sugar
8-9	cups flour, divided
2	eggs
1	tablespoon plus 2 teaspoons salt
1	pound (2 cups) butter or margarine, at room temperature

For Cinnamon Twists

butter or margarine for spreading, about 2-3 tablespoons
sugar and cinnamon for sprinkling

Proof the yeast by combining warm water, yeast and 1 tablespoon sugar. Stir to combine and let rest 5-10 minutes until it begins to foam. If it doesn't foam, start over with different yeast.

In a large mixing bowl, using the paddle beater, combine liquid, 1 cup sugar and yeast mixture. While mixer is running, add 5 cups flour. Beat until smooth and all flour is incorporated, but do not overbeat. Add eggs, salt and $1\frac{1}{2}$-2 cups more flour – just enough to make a thick batter, it should still flow out of the bowl. Pour into a floured 9x13-inch pan. Sprinkle flour on top, cover with plastic wrap and let rest at least one hour in the refrigerator. More than one hour is fine too.

Roll & Fold: 1) Uncover and pour dough out onto a well-floured pastry cloth. 2) Roll into a 12x18-inch rectangle. 3) Spread $\frac{1}{2}$ cup (1 stick) of butter on the bottom $\frac{2}{3}$ of the dough. 4) Fold down top $\frac{1}{3}$ of the dough then fold bottom $\frac{1}{3}$ up, overlapping the previous fold. 5) Then fold both ends into the center, without overlapping. 6) Fold one more time like closing a book. Rotate dough one quarter turn and repeat steps 2-6 three more times using remaining $1\frac{1}{2}$ cups butter.

Put back into floured 9x13-inch pan, dust top with flour and cover with plastic. Refrigerate at least one hour – longer is fine.

Divide dough into quarters. Using one quarter at a time, roll into a rectangle $\frac{1}{4}$-$\frac{1}{2}$ inch thick. At this point you can make Crescent rolls or Cinnamon Twist rolls.

Crescent Rolls: Cut dough into triangles. Roll into crescent shapes, starting with the widest side, and place on greased or parchment-covered cookie sheet. Cover loosely with plastic wrap.

Cinnamon Twist Rolls: Spread a thin layer of butter on the dough. Sprinkle sugar and cinnamon on the bottom half of the rectangle (about 1 tablespoon sugar and $\frac{1}{4}$ teaspoon cinnamon per quarter of dough). Fold top half of the dough onto the bottom half. Cut crosswise into one-inch strips. Pick each strip up by the ends, twist, and place on greased or parchment-covered cookie sheet. Cover loosely with plastic wrap.

Both Rolls: Let rise about 2 hours or until double in size. Remove plastic and bake at 375 degrees 13-15 minutes or until golden brown. Frost cinnamon rolls with powdered sugar frosting when cool.

3-5 dozen, depending on size

This dough can be refrigerated 4-5 days.

You can also fill the Cinnamon Twists with other fillings such as jams, pie fillings or Apricot Purée (see page 147).

A pastry cloth isn't necessary for this recipe, but it is much easier when using one.

This is the recipe that started my business and remains my trademark. I found it in the *Farm Journal Magazine* in 1970 and I've never seen another recipe quite like it in all the years I've been collecting. Sometimes things just work out.

Overnight Coffeecake

Easy, good and make-ahead — a great combination.

12-15 servings

~

You may have trouble with the topping sinking to the bottom of the cake overnight. If so, mix and refrigerate the batter overnight and sprinkle the topping on just before baking.

~

Inspiration: *Des Moines Register*, 1974

Cake

2	cups flour
1/2	teaspoon salt
1	teaspoon baking soda
1	teaspoon baking powder
3/4	cup margarine, softened
1/2	cup firmly packed light brown sugar
1/2	cup granulated sugar
2	eggs
1	teaspoon vanilla
1	cup buttermilk (or 1 cup milk with 1 tablespoon white vinegar)

Topping

1/2	cup firmly packed light brown sugar
1	teaspoon cinnamon
	a few grates of nutmeg, optional

Preheat oven to 350 degrees.

In a small bowl, combine flour, salt, baking soda and baking powder. Stir and set aside.

In a mixer bowl, cream margarine and sugars until light and fluffy. Add eggs and beat again to combine well. Add vanilla. Add flour mixture alternately with buttermilk—beginning and ending with flour mixture. Spread in a greased 9x13-inch pan.

Topping: Mix 1/2 cup brown sugar, cinnamon and nutmeg and sprinkle over batter in pan. Cover and refrigerate overnight or bake immediately in a 350-degree oven 30-35 minutes or until cake tests done.

Sticky Cinnamon Rolls, Cinnamon Bread & Cocktail Buns

This recipe is from my mother-in-law, Isabel.

Makes 9 sticky rolls, 1 loaf of cinnamon bread or 20-25 cocktail buns.

~

As you can see, this is the all-purpose sweet dough. It keeps in the refrigerator 3-4 days. In fact, the dough is easier to shape when it is cold, but it takes longer to rise after shaping. I have found that the rising after shaping is very important. If you let it rise too much, the sticky rolls seem to absorb the caramel and the cinnamon bread separates. Don't be afraid, just watch so they don't rise more than double.

Dough

1	cup warm water (105-110 degrees)
1	tablespoon active dry yeast
1/3	cup granulated sugar
1/4	cup solid vegetable shortening
3-3 1/2	cups all-purpose flour
1	egg
1 1/2	teaspoons salt

For Sticky Cinnamon Rolls

1/2	cup butter, melted
1/2	cup firmly packed light brown sugar
1/2	cup corn syrup (half dark and half light or all light)
	softened butter for spreading
1/2	cup firmly packed light brown sugar
1/2	teaspoon cinnamon

For Cinnamon Bread

	softened butter for spreading
1/3	cup granulated sugar
1/2	teaspoon cinnamon

For Cocktail Buns

	a few drops of yellow food coloring

In a mixer bowl, combine warm water, yeast and sugar. Let rest for 5-10 minutes to proof the yeast. It should be foamy and puffed up if the yeast is working.

Add shortening and 2 cups flour and mix with paddle beater until very smooth. (If you mix well at this stage, you are beginning to form the gluten necessary for a stable loaf of bread, which reduces the mixing time when you add the remaining flour.)

Add egg, salt and food coloring (if making cocktail buns). Slowly continue to add flour and mix until dough is elastic and pulls away from the sides of the bowl. Turn dough into a greased bowl, cover and let rest in a warm place until double in size (45 minutes-1 hour). Turn dough out onto a floured surface and shape and bake according to the recipe you want to make. OR punch the dough down, cover and refrigerate to use later.

Sticky Cinnamon Rolls: Combine melted butter, brown sugar and corn syrup. Spread in the bottom of a 9x13-inch pan. Turn dough out onto a floured surface. Press or roll into a rectangle about 12x8 inches. Spread with a thin layer of butter (to help hold the sugar in place). Top with 1/2 cup brown sugar and cinnamon. Starting from the long side, tightly roll up dough sealing well. Cut dough in 1 1/2-inch slices and place, cut-side down, in prepared pan. Cover loosely with plastic wrap and let rise until almost double (20-30 minutes if dough has not been chilled). Remove plastic and bake in a 350-degree oven on the lowest rack for 35-40 minutes, until brown and dough springs back when lightly touched. Immediately turn rolls out onto foil, letting caramel run down sides of the rolls.

Cinnamon Bread: Press or roll dough into a rectangle about 10x9 inches. Spread with a thin layer of butter. Sprinkle with granulated sugar and cinnamon. Starting at the short end, roll dough tightly sealing edges and ends and place in a greased 9x5-inch loaf pan. Cover loosely with plastic wrap and let rise until almost double. Uncover and bake in a 350-degree oven for 30-35 minutes, until brown and loaf sounds hollow when tapped lightly. Remove from pan and cool. Frost with powdered sugar frosting.

Cocktail Buns: Cut dough into small pieces, about the size of a golf ball. Shape into balls and place on a greased or parchment-covered cookie sheet about 1 inch apart. Cover loosely with plastic wrap and let rise until almost double (this only takes 20-30 minutes if the dough has not been chilled). Uncover and bake 12-15 minutes at 350 degrees, until golden brown. Remove from oven and rub tops with butter.

Rye–Carrot Bread

When you toast this, you think you are in aroma heaven.

2-3 loaves

I love giving small loaves of this as gifts. I bake them in small bowls I have around my kitchen and make 3-5 out of one recipe. It is great to have in the freezer for a special breakfast. One small loaf is about right for toast for one meal.

It can be tricky to get these cooked without getting them too brown. Try using three smaller loaf pans like the disposable aluminum pans if you want a loaf shape or just make smaller round loaves.

Inspiration: *Pillsbury Bake-Off Cookbook,* 1980

3/4	cup warm water (105-110 degrees)
3	tablespoons active dry yeast (3 packages)
1	teaspoon granulated sugar
1/4	teaspoon ground ginger
13/4	cups hot water
1	cup bran cereal (I like All Bran Buds)
1/2	cup firmly packed light brown sugar
1/3	cup light molasses
1/4	cup vegetable oil
1/2	cup packed shredded carrots
1	cup rye flour
1	tablespoon salt
5-6	cups all-purpose flour

In a small bowl, combine warm water, yeast, granulated sugar and ginger. Stir to dissolve yeast. Let rest 5-10 minutes until foamy.

In a large mixer bowl using the paddle beater, combine hot water, bran cereal, brown sugar, molasses and vegetable oil. Let rest about 5 minutes to soften the cereal. Add carrots and rye flour and mix to blend. Add yeast mixture, salt and 2 cups all purpose flour. Mix 2-3 minutes until very smooth. Gradually add more flour until dough is heavy and begins to pull away from the bowl. Turn dough out onto a floured surface and knead 1-2 minutes adding flour only when needed to prevent sticking. Place in a greased bowl and turn to get the greased side on top. Cover with plastic wrap and let rise until double in size (1-2 hours).

Turn dough out onto a floured surface and shape into 2 loaves. Place into greased 9x5-inch loaf pans. Cover and let rise again until almost double.

Preheat oven to 350 degrees.

Bake 35-45 minutes in the lower third of the oven until brown and loaf sounds hollow when lightly tapped. Cover loaves with foil if they start to get too brown. Remove from pan and rub tops with butter.

Crunchy Bread

This is a great alternative to garlic bread.

1	loaf French bread, cut in 1-inch slices
3/4	cup butter or margarine
1/2	teaspoon celery seed
1/2	teaspoon paprika

Preheat oven to 375 degrees.

Combine butter, celery seed and paprika. Spread on both sides of bread slices. Place on cookie sheet. Bake 20 minutes. Turn slices over after 10 minutes for maximum crispiness. However, I've made this many times without turning.

6-8 servings

~

If you want to make this extra fancy, cut off all the crust and butter all edges.

~

Inspiration: *Better Homes & Gardens,* 1975

Pull-Apart Cheese Bread

3/4	cup grated Romano or Parmesan cheese
1/2	teaspoon garlic powder
1/2	teaspoon paprika
2	tablespoons sesame seeds
1/2	cup plus 2 tablespoons butter or margarine, melted, divided
1	recipe sweet roll dough (page 72) – using half the sugar

If using sweet roll dough, mix and let rise once.

Combine cheese, garlic powder, paprika and sesame seeds in a small bowl. Pour 1/2 cup melted butter into the bottom of a 9x13-inch pan and sprinkle with half the cheese mixture.

Cut sweet dough or thawed dough into small pieces, about the size of a walnut. Place in prepared pan, leaving a 1/2-inch space between pieces for rising. Pour remaining 2 tablespoons butter over the dough and sprinkle with remaining cheese mixture.

Cover pan with plastic wrap and let dough rise until almost double in size. Preheat oven to 350 degrees. Bake 20-25 minutes, until lightly brown and bread in the middle of the pan springs back when lightly touched. Remove from oven, gently loosen edges with knife and turn out onto serving plate.

Note: This can also be made with 1 loaf of frozen bread dough, thawed, but reduce the butter to 1/3 cup plus 2 tablespoons.

10-12 servings

~

This can be served all in one piece and each person pulls off a piece or break it up and serve in a bread basket.

Rotini in Red Butter Sauce

This recipe is rich, wonderful and easy!

12	ounces rotini, cooked in salted water
1/2	cup butter
2-4	cloves garlic, finely minced
2	cups heavy cream
1/4	cup tomato paste
1 1/2	teaspoons sweet, Hungarian paprika
1	teaspoon leaf sage, crumbled
	salt to taste
	Romano cheese

Melt butter in a large saucepan over medium-high heat. Add garlic and cook for about 1 minute. Add cream and tomato paste. Cook (watch carefully because it boils over easily) until cream is reduced about half and slightly thick (5-7 minutes). Stir in paprika, sage and salt. Pour sauce over pasta and top with Romano cheese.

Adding cooked chicken would make a quick supper dish.

6-8 first-course servings

I have used tomato sauce when I didn't have paste. It worked fine, just a little less intense tomato flavor.

Inspiration: Corning Ware ad in *Bon Appétit*, 1983

Pasta and Vegetables in Garlic Sauce

This is such a colorful dish.

1	(9-ounce) package refrigerated fettuccine
2	carrots, cut into thin strips*
2	zucchini, cut into thin strips*
1/4	cup butter
1	medium onion, chopped
2	cloves garlic, minced
1/2	cup chicken broth
1/2	cup heavy cream
	salt to taste
1/2	cup Romano cheese

Cook fettuccine in a large pan of salted water for about 1 minute. Add carrot and zucchini strips and continue to cook another 2-3 minutes, mixing in the vegetables with the pasta. A large meat fork works great. Drain pasta and vegetables and set aside.

In the same pan, melt butter. Add onion and sauté until translucent. Add garlic and heat until garlic becomes fragrant but not brown. Add broth and cream. Cook until slightly thickened. Add the pasta mix to the sauce and toss to coat. Taste for seasoning. Add Romano cheese just before serving.

3-4 servings

* Using a vegetable peeler on both the carrots and zucchini makes long shreds about the same width as the fettuccine. Make zucchini shreds using the green outside and just a few shreds of the white part. Don't use the seedy middle.

Inspiration: Pillsbury cookbooks

Pasta Shells with Three Cheeses

A great "macaroni" and cheese dish with a few extras.

8	ounces medium pasta shells
3	tablespoons butter
1/2	cup sliced green onions
2	cloves garlic, minced
1	small shallot, chopped
1/2	cup finely diced green pepper
1/2	cup finely diced red pepper
3	ounces cream cheese
1	cup chicken broth
1	cup heavy cream
4	ounces provolone cheese, shredded (1 cup)
4	ounces Monterey Jack cheese, shredded (1 cup)
3/4	cup fresh bread crumbs mixed with 1 tablespoon melted butter, optional

Cook pasta in lots of salted water until al dente – don't overcook it because you will bake it later. Drain and place in a greased 2-quart or 7x11-inch baking dish.

Preheat oven to 400 degrees.

In a large saucepan, melt butter and sauté green onions, garlic, shallot and peppers until vegetables are soft (about 2 minutes). Add cream cheese and stir until it begins to melt. Add chicken broth, cream and shredded cheeses. Stir over low heat until cheeses melt. Pour over pasta and top with buttered bread crumbs.

Cover with foil and bake 30 minutes or until bubbly. Remove foil and bake another 5 minutes or so to brown the crumbs.

4-6 servings

~

This recipe was in an article highlighting the food processor, so all the vegetables were chopped in the processor. This works great, but I still chop the green onion with a knife.

~

Inspired by: *Bon Appétit*, 1986

French Rice

Just a little zip to a rice dish.

¼	cup butter or margarine
1	cup uncooked rice (I like to use converted rice)
1	(10¾-ounce) can French onion soup, plus enough water to equal 2 cups
1	(4-ounce) can sliced mushrooms, drained
1	(8-ounce) can sliced water chestnuts, drained

Preheat oven to 350 degrees.

In a greased 1½-quart casserole dish, melt butter in the microwave. (You can also do this in a pan on the stove, but why dirty a pan?) Add remaining ingredients, stirring to combine. Cover and bake at 350 degrees for one hour, or until rice is done. Stir before serving.

Brown Rice with Mushrooms, Sour Cream & Jack Cheese

This is rich but yummy. Also holds its heat well for a great pot luck dish.

2	cups beef broth
1	cup short grain brown rice
8	ounces sliced fresh mushrooms
3	tablespoons butter or margarine
½	cup minced onion
2	cloves garlic, minced
1	cup sour cream
6	ounces Monterey Jack cheese, shredded (1½ cups)

Boil broth in a medium saucepan. Add rice, cover and bring to a boil again. Reduce heat and simmer until rice is tender, about 1 hour.

Preheat oven to 400 degrees.

Cook mushrooms and butter in a skillet over medium-high heat until mushrooms begin to give up their juices. Add onion and garlic and continue to cook and stir 2-3 minutes until onions are translucent and you can smell the garlic. Remove from heat, add sour cream and rice. Stir to combine.

Turn the rice mixture into a greased, shallow casserole dish, about 1½ quarts. (You don't want a deep rice mixture because you are going to put the cheese on top and you want to be able to get cheese and rice with every spoonful.) Sprinkle cheese on top of rice mixture. Cover and bake 15-20 minutes or until heated through and cheese is melted. It will take longer if it has been refrigerated (25-35 minutes).

8 servings

If you don't have French onion soup, you can use beef soup base and minced, dried onions. Start with 2 cups of water and add 1 tablespoon of soup base and 3-4 tablespoons of minced, dried onions.

Inspiration: *Southern Living*

6-8 generous servings

This dish is very easy to make ahead and heat for service.

Inspiration: *Gourmet*, 1984

Green Bean & Almond Rice

The red pepper is very important in this recipe — both for taste and color. Pictured on page 90.

Pictured on page 90.

6-8 servings

2	cups beef broth
1	cup short grain brown rice
4	tablespoons butter or margarine
¾	cup chopped red pepper
¾	cup chopped onion
10	ounces frozen, french-style green beans
½	cup toasted slivered almonds

Boil broth in a small saucepan with a tight fitting lid. Add rice, cover and bring back to a boil. Turn down heat and simmer for 1 hour or until done. Taste to determine how done you like it.

In a microwave-safe bowl, combine butter, red pepper and onion. Cook on high power for 2 minutes or until vegetables are soft or sauté in a frying pan until onions are translucent and peppers are cooked.

Cook green beans in lightly salted water as directed on package. Drain. Combine rice, onion mixture and green beans. Add almonds and serve.

Using beef broth rather than water to cook the rice really makes a difference. If you are concerned about the amount of salt in the broth, use less beef base to start then add more at the end, to your taste. I have also discovered it is very difficult to cook less than 1 cup of brown rice at one time. So if you don't want this much rice, cook it up anyway and freeze any rice you don't use.

Rice with Dried Cranberries, Green Onions & Pine Nuts

4-6 servings

I use a combination of rice – more white than brown, more brown than wild; about a 3-2-1 ratio. I always cook brown rice in beef broth.

6	tablespoons butter or margarine
1	bunch green onions, sliced (about ¾ cup)
3	cups cooked rice (about 1½ cups uncooked), you can use white rice, brown rice, wild rice or a combination
¾	cup dried cranberries
½	cup pine nuts or toasted slivered almonds (optional)

In a medium bowl, microwave butter and onion until onions are soft (about 2 minutes). Add remaining ingredients, cover with plastic wrap and microwave until heated through (2-3 minutes). This can also be heated in a pan on the stove.

Barley Casserole

4-6 servings

6	tablespoons butter or margarine
¼	cup sliced green onions
2	cups chicken or beef broth
1	cup medium pearl barley, rinsed & drained
¼	cup chopped parsley, optional
½	cup toasted slivered almonds, optional

Preheat oven to 350 degrees.

In a 1½-quart casserole dish, microwave butter and onions about 2 minutes to soften onions. (This can also be done in a frying pan on the stove.) Add broth and barley. Cover and bake 1 hour. Uncover, stir in parsley and almonds and return to oven until all moisture is absorbed (about 10 minutes). Stir and serve.

Fried Pasta with Smoked Beef & Sun Dried Tomatoes, page 17

81

*Gallettes of Dried Beef &
Provolone with Fresh Spinach
Sauce, page 18*

*Cornish Hen with Sausage & Mushroom
Stuffing, page 46*

82

Salmon Napoleons, page 12

This is such a simple recipe, I want everyone to try it!
This picture shows all the steps to preparing this dish.

1. *frozen, uncooked puff pastry*
2 & 3. *baked pastry, divided*
4. *thinly sliced salmon on pastry*
5. *baked and reassembled salmon and pastry,*
   ready to be sliced
6 *ready to serve, complete with Buerre Blanc sauce*

Soup under Wraps, page 7;
Tomato Soup, page 6;
Spinach Soup, page 6

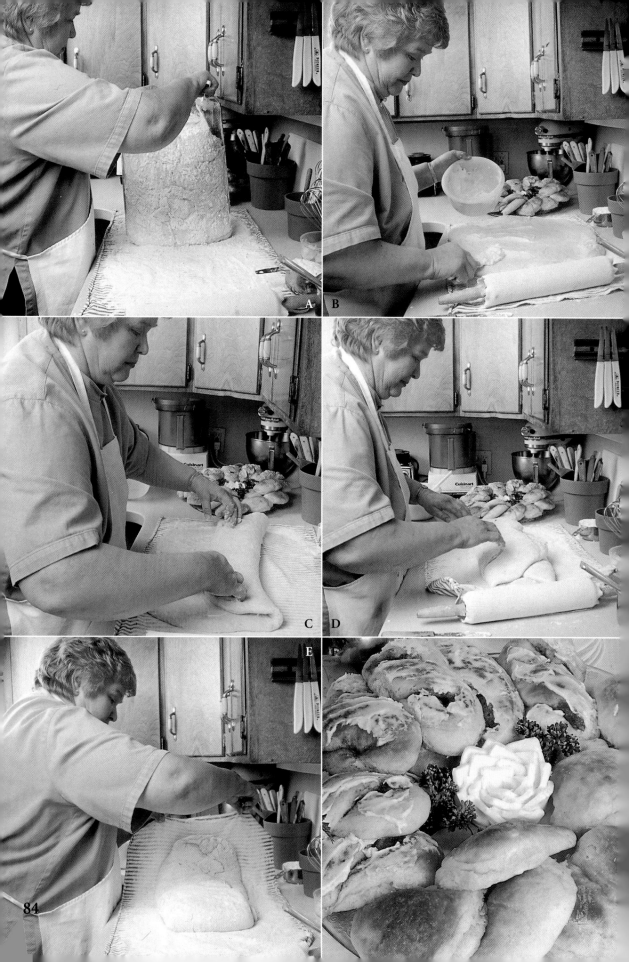

84

Crescent Rolls & Cinnamon Twist Danish

The pictures show a doubled batch of dough.

1	cup warm water (105-110 degrees)
3	tablespoons yeast (or 3 packages)
1	tablespoon sugar
2	cups liquid (milk, water or half of each)
1	cup sugar
8-9	cups flour, divided
2	eggs
1	tablespoon plus 2 teaspoons salt
1	pound (2 cups) butter or margarine, at room temperature

For Cinnamon Twists

butter or margarine for spreading, about 2-3 tablespoons
sugar and cinnamon for sprinkling

Proof the yeast by combining warm water, yeast and 1 tablespoon sugar. Stir to combine and let rest 5-10 minutes until it begins to foam. If it doesn't foam, start over with different yeast.

In a large mixing bowl, using the paddle beater, combine liquid, 1 cup sugar and yeast mixture. While mixer is running, add 5 cups flour. Beat until smooth and all flour is incorporated, but do not overbeat. Add eggs, salt and $1\frac{1}{2}$-2 cups more flour – just enough to make a thick batter, it should still flow out of the bowl. Pour into a floured 9x13-inch pan. Sprinkle flour on top, cover with plastic wrap and let rest at least one hour in the refrigerator. More than one hour is fine too.

Roll & Fold: 1) Uncover and pour dough out onto a well-floured pastry cloth (photo A). 2) Roll into a 12x18-inch rectangle. 3) Spread $\frac{1}{2}$ cup (1 stick) of butter on the bottom $\frac{2}{3}$ of the dough (photo B). 4) Fold down top $\frac{1}{3}$ of the dough then fold bottom $\frac{1}{3}$ up, overlapping the previous fold (photos C & D). 5) Then fold both ends into the center, without overlapping (photo E). 6) Fold one more time like closing a book. Rotate dough one quarter turn and repeat steps 2-6 three more times using remaining $1\frac{1}{2}$ cups butter.

Put back into floured 9x13-inch pan, dust top with flour and cover with plastic. Refrigerate at least one hour – longer is fine.

Divide dough into quarters. Using one quarter at a time, roll into a rectangle $\frac{1}{4}$-$\frac{1}{2}$ inch thick. At this point you can make Crescent rolls or Cinnamon Twist rolls.

Crescent Rolls: Cut dough into triangles. Roll into crescent shapes, starting with the widest side, and place on greased or parchment-covered cookie sheet. Cover loosely with plastic wrap.

Cinnamon Twist Rolls: Spread a thin layer of butter on the dough. Sprinkle sugar and cinnamon on the bottom half of the rectangle (about 1 tablespoon sugar and $\frac{1}{4}$ teaspoon cinnamon per quarter of dough). Fold top half of the dough onto the bottom half. Cut crosswise into one-inch strips. Pick each strip up by the ends, twist, and place on greased or parchment-covered cookie sheet. Cover loosely with plastic wrap.

Both Rolls: Let rise about 2 hours or until double in size. Remove plastic and bake at 375 degrees 13-15 minutes or until golden brown. Frost cinnamon rolls with powdered sugar frosting when cool.

3-5 dozen, depending on size

~

This dough can be refrigerated 4-5 days.

~

You can also fill the Cinnamon Twists with other fillings such as jams, pie fillings or Apricot Purée (see page 147).

~

A pastry cloth isn't necessary for this recipe, but it is much easier when using one.

~

This is the recipe that started my business and remains my trademark. I found it in the *Farm Journal Magazine* in 1970 and I've never seen another recipe quite like it in all the years I've been collecting. Sometimes things just work out.

85

Spinach-Stuffed Chicken, page 54

Chicken with Pastrami, Spinach and Cheese, page 53

Hearts of Palm & Black Bean Salad, page 29; Chicken in Puff Pastry, page 60; Sweet & Sour Carrots, page 98

87

Timbales of Crab
& Spinach Mousse, page 13

Gateâu Florentine, page 48;
Surprise Combination Salad,
page 35

Spinach-Stuffed Onions, page 106; Beef with Wine Sauce, page 39; Oven Roasted Potatoes, page 113

Pork Tenderloin Tournedos, page 44;
Green Bean Almond Rice, page 79;
Julienne Vegetables with Lemon
Butter Sauce, page 100

Puff Pastry Pears,
page 142

Puff Pastry Pears
from above.

*Warm Chocolate Cake
with a Soft Heart, page 121*

*Clockwise from top: Oatmeal Shortbread,
page 159; Eskimo Balls, page 157; Napoleon
Creams, page 152; Salted Nut Bars, page 157;
Buckeyes, page 156; Chocolate Hazelnut
Torte, page 117; Chocolate Mint Bars, 160*

Top: Chocolate Hazelnut Torte, page 117; Bottom: Chocolate Praline Cake, page 120

93

Clockwise from top: Chocolate Marble Cheesecake, page 132; Blackberry Cheesecake, page 131; Lemon Curd Cheesecake, page 133; Raspberry Swirl Cheesecake, page 130; Sour Cream Cheesecake, page 129

Foreground: Pecan Cream Pie, page 137; Background: Lace Oatmeal Cookies, page 159; Strawberry Cream Pie filling, page 136

*Meringue Pie Shells, page 134;
Fillings (clockwise from top): White
Chocolate Strawberry, page 134;
Lemon, page 135; Chocolate Toffee,
page 135*

*Left: Toasted Almond Bavarian with
Raspberry Sauce, page 140
Below: Devil's Mousse Cake with
Crème de Cacao Cream, page 119*

95

On the left is the formal living room in our country home decorated for Christmas. The stockings are hanging for our children. You'll notice the two on the left have additional names for grandchildren. On the right is the guest book that we ask our guests to sign. People from all over the world - Japan, South America, Europe - amazingly find their way to a farm house in the middle of Iowa. Also pictured are menus from which our guests select their meal prior to coming to our home.

This is the dining room in our home. The table is set for a Christmas-time dinner. The home was built in 1919 and includes a built-in oak buffet, oak beams and plate rails. I have taken my job of filling the plate rails very seriously!

This is the kitchen in our home. There have been no major changes to accommodate the restaurant. The left photo is the "dream world" kitchen, rarely seen in this condition. The right photo is the "real world" kitchen taken on the first day of our food photo shoot.

Vegetables

Sweet & Sour Carrots

4-5 servings

~

I slice the onion lengthwise so they have the appearance of shreds, like the carrots.

~

Carrots have differing degrees of sweetness. That's why it is hard to determine how much red wine vinegar to add until you have tasted the carrots.

I love these carrots with chicken or pork. Pictured on page 87.

2	tablespoons butter
1/2	medium onion, sliced lengthwise
1	pound carrots, shredded
1/2	cup currant jelly
2-3	tablespoons water
	salt to taste
	red wine vinegar to taste

In a medium saucepan over medium-high heat, melt butter. Add onion and sauté until translucent, but not brown. Add carrots, jelly and water. Cover and cook over medium heat, stirring often, until carrots are tender (5-10 minutes). I actually like these carrots a little overdone, so I cook them a little longer.

Season with salt then taste for sweetness. Add red wine vinegar, 1 teaspoon at a time, until they taste good to you. Sometimes I don't add any vinegar, depending on the carrots.

Baby Carrots with Mustard & Brown Sugar Glaze

8-10 servings

~

I like to use coarse ground mustard because it gives the carrots a texture that looks great.

~

Inspiration: *McCall's* general cookbook, 1963

2	pounds baby carrots
1/4	cup butter
1/2	cup firmly packed light brown sugar
1/4	cup mustard (I use coarse ground mustard)

Cook carrots in water seasoned with salt and sugar until tender. Drain. In the same saucepan, melt butter and add brown sugar and mustard. Continue to cook 3-5 minutes until glaze is syrupy. Add carrots and stir to coat. Serve immediately. (The glaze tends to get watered down if you add the carrots too soon before service.)

98

Carrots & Apricots

4	tablespoons butter
1	medium onion, cut in thin strips
1	pound carrots, shredded
3	ounces California dried apricots, cut in thin strips
½	cup water
	salt to taste

Melt butter in medium skillet or saucepan over medium-high heat. Add onion and cook until soft but not brown. Add carrots, apricots and water. Stir, then cover and cook until carrots are tender (5-10 minutes). Uncover, salt to taste and cook until most of the liquid evaporates, stirring occasionally.

4-6 servings

Cutting the onion in thin strips makes them blend in better with the shredded carrots and apricots.

Inspiration: *Bon Appétit*, 1980

Carrot & Apple Purée

People won't take big servings of this.

2	pounds carrots, sliced in 1-inch pieces
1	tablespoon vegetable oil
4	tart apples (I use Granny Smith), peeled, cored and cut in quarters
2	tablespoons butter
	salt to taste

Preheat oven to 350 degrees.

Place carrots on a jelly roll pan and sprinkle with vegetable oil; stir to coat. Cover pan with foil and bake at 350 degrees for 1 hour.

Remove from oven and add apple quarters. Cover, return to oven and bake 15-20 minutes more until apples and carrots are very soft. Remove from oven and put into food processor fitted with the chopping blade. Process until smooth. (You can also do this in a blender, but you might have to divide it into two batches.) Stir in butter and season with salt.

8-10 servings

If the purée is too liquid, put it in a pan and heat carefully, stirring once in a while, until some of the liquid evaporates.

This is very easy to make ahead. Put in an oven-proof bowl and bake, covered, until heated through.

Julienne Vegetables with Lemon Butter Sauce

You will be surprised how well this combination goes together. People will eat this who would never eat turnips or rutabaga. Pictured on page 90.

Pictured on page 90.

1-2	tablespoons salt
1-2	tablespoons sugar
2½	cups julienne carrots
2	cups julienne rutabaga
1	cup julienne turnips
3	tablespoons butter
2	tablespoons fresh lemon juice

Fill a large saucepan halfway with water. Add 1-2 tablespoons salt and an equal amount of sugar. Bring to a boil and add carrots and rutabaga. Bring back to a boil and cook 2-3 minutes, then add turnips. Bring back to a boil and cook 2-3 minutes more until vegetables are tender. The turnips should look translucent when they are ready. They continue to cook a little after they are drained. Drain. Return to saucepan and add butter and lemon juice. Continue to heat gently until butter melts and excess water evaporates, 2-3 minutes.

4-6 servings

The proportions of carrots to rutabagas and turnips is, of course, up to you, but I've found it goes over better if there are more carrots than any other vegetable.

Try to cut the vegetables the same size. The carrots and rutabaga cook at about the same rate.

Rainbow of Four Vegetables with Hollandaise Sauce

This recipe looks complicated but it is basically four vegetables cooked separately then layered in a ramekin.

2	eggs
2	egg yolks
1	cup heavy cream
2	tablespoons plus 2 teaspoons fresh lemon juice, divided
1	pound carrots, sliced
4	cups loosely packed broccoli florets
1½	pounds turnips, peeled and sliced
12	ounces mushrooms, chopped
2	tablespoons oil

Combine eggs, egg yolks, cream and 2 tablespoons lemon juice. Set aside.

Cook separately in salted water, carrots, broccoli and turnips until very well done. Drain well. Put carrots in blender or food processor. Blend until smooth. To help blend, pour in ¼ of the egg yolk mixture (about ⅓ cup). Divide the puréed carrots among 8 greased 5-6-ounce ramekins. Circles of parchment paper placed in the bottom of the greased ramekins are helpful when unmolding but not necessary. Repeat the purée process with the broccoli, then turnips, adding ⅓ cup egg yolk mixture to each vegetable. I add a little extra lemon juice to the turnip purée, up to 2 teaspoons for a little extra taste.

Preheat oven to 325 degrees.

Sauté mushrooms with oil until they begin to brown and release their moisture (3-5 minutes). Cool slightly. Sprinkle with a little salt. Add remaining egg yolk mixture to mushrooms and spoon on top of the turnip purée in ramekins.

Put ramekins in cake pan and fill pan with hot water about halfway up the sides of ramekins. Cover with foil. Bake 35-40 minutes until top layer looks set. Remove from oven and water bath. Let rest 5-10 minutes.

To unmold, loosen edges with knife, turn out onto serving plates and remove parchment circle. Serve with Hollandaise sauce or a lemon butter sauce.

Hollandaise Sauce

4	egg yolks
2	tablespoons fresh lemon juice
3	tablespoons hot water
½	cup butter, at room temperature

In a small, heavy saucepan or top of a double boiler mix egg yolks, lemon juice and hot water. Heat gently, whisking constantly, until mixture begins to thicken. Reduce heat and whisk in butter. Don't let it get too hot while whisking in the butter.

8 servings

These can be made up to one day ahead and refrigerated. Either bring them up to room temperature before baking or increase baking time by about 10 minutes.

I have found that it is easier to cook each vegetable one at a time, using the same pan. You can purée each vegetable while the next one is cooking and you don't dirty as many dishes.

Inspiration:
Bon Appétit, 1981

Norwegian Stir-Fry Broccoli & Carrots

I like this over rice for a meatless lunch.

4-6 servings

~

I learned the blanching trick when I had to make this for a large group. I didn't have time to stand and stir fry the vegetables until they were crisp-tender because of the quantity needed. So I had to come up with a way to get the same result without the fuss. This works great.

~

The lemon makes the broccoli turn a little brown, so add it at the very end. You may want to add more or less for your taste.

~

Inspiration: *Betty Crocker International Cookbook*, 1986

2	cups small (in diameter) carrots, sliced 1/4 inch thick
2	cups bite-size broccoli florets
2	tablespoons vegetable oil
1	bunch green onions, sliced using some of the green (about 3/4 cup)
2	thin slices of gingerroot, finely chopped
1-2	cloves garlic, minced
2	cups chicken broth
1	(8-ounce) can sliced water chestnuts, drained
2	tablespoons oyster sauce
2	tablespoons cornstarch
1-2	tablespoons fresh lemon juice

Fill a medium to large saucepan half full with water. Add salt to taste. Heat to boiling and add carrots. Boil 1-2 minutes then add broccoli. Boil 1-2 minutes more. Drain and rinse with cold water to stop the cooking.

It is a good idea to have the rest of the ingredients ready, because it goes very fast from this point. In a large skillet over high heat, heat oil then add green onions, gingerroot and garlic. Stir 30-60 seconds then add chicken broth, water chestnuts and oyster sauce. Combine corn starch and 2 tablespoons cold water and gradually stir into hot mixture until broth thickens to about the same thickness as caramel topping. Add the vegetables, stirring to cover with sauce and heat until warm. Just before serving, add lemon juice and stir once more.

Broccoli with Orange Shallot Butter

1½-2	bunches peeled broccoli spears (That is the floret plus 2-3 inches of the joining branch. I usually plan on 4-5 servings from a bunch of broccoli. In our grocery store, there are usually 2-3 stalks per bunch.)
1	medium to large shallot, chopped (about 3 tablespoons)
½	cup butter
½	cup orange juice concentrate, cold or even frozen

To peel broccoli, hold the broccoli spear by the floret end and with a paring knife start at the stalk end and strip the tough outer skin from the stalk up to the floret. This takes a little getting used to but once you eat broccoli prepared this way you won't like it any other way.

To cook, bring a pot of salted water to a boil. Add broccoli spears, return to a boil and cook 2-3 minutes. Drain & keep warm*.

For butter sauce: In a small saucepan over medium-high heat, combine shallots and butter. Sauté for a minute or two. Whisk in the orange juice and heat through — do not overheat or it will break the butter. The sauce should be slightly thick, like corn syrup. Pour over broccoli just before serving.

To prepare broccoli ahead of time, follow directions through cooking. Drain and immediately rinse or submerge in icy cold water until cool. Arrange cooled, drained broccoli in serving dish — preferably a microwavable and oven-proof dish. Cover with plastic wrap and refrigerate. This can be done the day before serving. When it is time to serve, microwave 2-4 minutes to heat up the broccoli. Then remove plastic wrap and place it in the oven (if you already have it on for something else) for 5 minutes to warm up the serving dish to keep the broccoli warm a little longer, especially if you are having a buffet.

When my girls read this recipe they said this was "way more" than they wanted to know about cooking broccoli, so take it for what it's worth.

6-8 servings

*My favorite way to cook broccoli spears is to start with a pan of boiling salted water deep enough to hold the largest spears upright. When the water is boiling, place spears, stem end down, into the water and ideally the floret end remains above the water. Continue to add all the broccoli spears, largest ones first. Then fill in with the smaller stems. When the floret turns dark green, boil about 30 seconds more then drain.

Inspiration:
Bon Appétit, 1984

Peas with Broccoli Medallions

4-6 servings

2   tablespoons vegetable oil
1/2-1   cup broccoli stems, peeled & thinly sliced, crosswise into rounds
1/2   cup green onions, sliced with some of the green tops
1   (10-ounce) package frozen peas
1/4   cup water
       salt to taste
1   tablespoon fresh lemon juice or to taste

Heat vegetable oil in a medium skillet over medium-high heat. Add broccoli stems and green onions. Cook and stir until broccoli medallions are partially cooked (2-3 minutes). Watch carefully so stems don't burn. Add peas and water. Stir, then cover and cook until peas are tender (3-5 minutes). Sprinkle with salt. Add lemon juice just before serving.

If you have never peeled broccoli stems, you can use a vegetable peeler or a paring knife. The tough skin pulls off quite easily and the stems become wonderful to cook or eat raw. I've used them on vegetable trays and often people have no idea what they are.

Inspiration:
Bon Appétit, 1981

Country French Peas

Every recipe I've seen called "Country French" peas has lettuce in it. This one also has bacon and caramelized sugar.

4-6   slices bacon, chopped
1   tablespoon butter or margarine
2   tablespoons sugar
10   ounces frozen peas
1   cup lightly packed, shredded Iceberg lettuce
1/4   teaspoon salt
1   tablespoon cornstarch, mixed with 1 tablespoon water

In a medium frying pan, fry bacon until brown and slightly crisp. Drain and set aside.

Wipe out the frying pan to remove dark bacon bits and excess grease. Add butter and sugar and cook over medium heat until sugar melts and becomes a light caramel color, stirring occasionally. Carefully add peas (because the melted sugar is very hot and the peas are frozen). Top with lettuce, salt and bacon. Pour 1/2 cup water over all and cover. Cook until peas are tender (6-8 minutes), stirring once or twice. Taste for seasoning — you might need more salt. There should be some liquid remaining on the peas. If not, add a little water. Carefully add the cornstarch-water mixture and bring to a boil to thicken the juice just enough to cling to the peas.

4-6 servings

The amount of sugar is personal. Add more or less to your own taste.

Inspiration: *The Bakery Cookbook*

Snappy Green Beans

This is our favorite way to have beans, when we don't have fresh.

1/2   pound bacon, diced
1   small onion, sliced
1/2   cup red wine vinegar
1-2   teaspoons seasoned salt
1   (16-ounce) package frozen French-style green beans

In a medium skillet over medium-high heat, fry bacon until partially cooked. Drain off some of the fat, but not all. Add onion and continue to cook until bacon is brown and onion is translucent. Add vinegar and seasoned salt — start with 1 teaspoon, then add more to taste after you add it to the beans. Continue to cook until most of the vinegar has cooked down. Remove from heat.

In a large saucepan, cook beans in 1/2 cup water, covered, until done (5-7 minutes). Do not drain. Add bacon mixture and cook for another five minutes or so, to develop flavors. Do not cover, so some of the liquid evaporates and there is very little liquid left at serving time.

6-8 servings

Inspiration: *Good Housekeeping*, 1970

Onion Fritters

This is for you, Cynthia & Suzanne!

1   cup Bisquick mix
1   tablespoon sugar
1/4   teaspoon salt
6   tablespoons water
2 1/2   cups finely chopped onion
     oil for frying, vegetable or canola

Combine Bisquick, sugar and salt. Add water and mix just until moistened. Stir in onion. The onion will make the batter more moist, that is why you don't want to add too much water in the beginning.

Fill 1/3 of a heavy saucepan with oil. A tall pan is safer for deep frying. Heat oil to 365-370 degrees. Using a soup spoon or other small spoon, drop level spoonfuls of batter into the oil. I found that smaller fritters are easier to cook all the way through without getting too brown. Turn over when they get brown on one side. This doesn't take very long. Test one fritter to be sure it is cooked. You might have to reduce the temperature of the oil to 360 degrees if they get too brown or make smaller fritters. Repeat with remaining batter. Drain on paper towels & keep warm in a 200-degree oven.

Makes 2 dozen small fritters

Be very careful when you deep fry. Even the bubbles can start a fire if they go over the pan.

Inspiration: *Farm Bureau Spokesman*, 1975

Spinach-Stuffed Onions

Pictured on page 89.

6 servings

* If you have a 3-ounce package of cream cheese, use that. If you have an 8 ounce package, use half of it. This is just to make it easy on your measuring.

** To make soft bread crumbs, break bread into a few large pieces and put into food processor or blender for a few seconds.

Inspiration: *Better Homes & Gardens,* 1971

2-3	large white onions
3-4	ounces cream cheese*
1	egg
1/4	cup milk
1	(10-ounce) package frozen, chopped spinach, thawed and squeezed dry
3/4	cup soft bread crumbs (1-2 slices bread)**
1/4	cup grated Romano cheese
1/4	teaspoon salt or to taste

Preheat oven to 350 degrees.

Remove all tough outer skin from onions. Remove root and stem ends of the onions by cutting a cone-shaped piece to get all of the root so the onion comes apart. Cut onion in half horizontally (around the equator, so to speak). Carefully loosen the rings of onion starting from the outer edge. You will need six onion cups, plus 2-3 extra cups to fill the holes in the bottoms of the onions. Put all onion cups in a microwavable dish, add 2 tablespoons water, cover with plastic wrap and microwave 1-2 minutes or until onion cups are softened a little. Remove from microwave. Tear the "extra" onion cups into pieces. Place torn pieces in the bottoms of the other 6 onion cups to cover the holes, then place in greased baking dish.

In a mixer or food processor, combine cream cheese, egg and milk. Process to combine. Add spinach, bread crumbs and Romano cheese. Process again. Add salt and taste for seasoning.

Fill onion cups with spinach mixture – about 1/4 cup per onion. You can also sprinkle some additional bread crumbs on top if desired. Cover pan with foil and bake 30-40 minutes, until spinach is set. If you have crumbs on top, remove foil and cook about 5 minutes more to brown crumbs.

Spinach Strudel

This looks fancy, tastes good and is easy to make. I serve this with Hollandaise Sauce (page 101).

¾	cup chopped onion
1	tablespoon margarine
2	(10-ounce) packages of frozen, chopped spinach, thawed and squeezed dry
½	pound bacon, chopped, cooked until crisp and drained
½	(8-ounce) can water chestnuts, chopped
12	ounces cream cheese, softened
1	tablespoon fresh lemon juice
½	teaspoon salt
6	sheets phyllo dough (about ⅓ of a 16-ounce package) melted margarine, approximately ½ cup

Preheat oven to 400 degrees.

Combine onion and margarine. Sauté over medium heat or microwave in a small bowl until onions are translucent.

Combine spinach, onion, bacon, water chestnuts, cream cheese, lemon juice and salt. Work the ingredients together. I think hands work best for this.

On a flat surface, unfold six sheets of phyllo dough. Taking one sheet at a time, brush melted margarine on each sheet and place it on top of the previous sheet. Spread spinach mixture in a line along the long edge of the dough leaving about 1-inch at each end. Roll the spinach up in the dough, tucking in the ends. You should have a long cylinder-shaped roll with spinach filling inside.

Place onto well-greased or parchment-covered cookie sheet, seam side down. Brush with melted margarine. Bake 30 minutes or until dough is golden brown. Using a serrated knife, slice into serving pieces. Servings have a better appearance if each piece is at least 1½ inches wide and sliced at an angle. Slicing can be tricky because dough flakes easily!

6 servings

~

You can make this ahead, cover with plastic wrap and put in the refrigerator for several hours. If you do, bake at 350 degrees for 35-45 minutes. Watch for the dough to turn golden brown.

~

Inspiration: *Betty Crocker Plain & Fancy Vegetables*, 1986

Scrambled Cabbage

One of the few low-fat recipes in this book!

4-6 servings

If you like your vegetables a little softer, add ½ cup water before you add the sugar, salt and vinegar and cook, stirring constantly until most of the water evaporates. Then add sugar, salt and vinegar.

2-3	tablespoons vegetable oil
3	cups shredded green cabbage
1	cup thinly sliced celery
½	cup chopped peppers (any color you wish, it's nice to have a variety)
1	medium onion, thinly sliced
1	teaspoon sugar
1	teaspoon salt
2-3	tablespoons white vinegar

Heat oil in a large skillet over medium heat. Add cabbage, celery, peppers and onion and cook, stirring constantly, until crisp-tender (about 5 minutes). Add sugar, salt and vinegar. Turn heat to high and stir for about 1 minute. Remove from heat and serve. Be careful not to keep it on high heat very long or the vegetables will burn.

Creamy Cabbage Packets with Bacon & Onion

This is a special presentation for an everyday vegetable.

8-10 servings

~

These can be made the day before and refrigerated, adding 5-10 minutes to the baking time.

~

Inspiration: *Bon Appétit*, 1996

1	large head green cabbage
1/2	pound bacon, cut into 2-inch julienne strips
1	large onion, cut in half — root to stem and then julienne strips
1	cup heavy cream, divided
1/2-1	teaspoon dried sage leaves, crumbled or 1 tablespoon chopped fresh (or to taste)

Using a sharp knife, remove core from center of cabbage by making a deep cone-shape cut. In a pan large enough to hold the cabbage head, heat enough water to cover cabbage. Bring water to a boil and add 2 tablespoons salt. Add the whole cabbage and cook until outer leaves soften and are easy to pull away from head. Remove the loose, soft outer leaves from the water. Continue to cook & pull off soft leaves until you have 8-10 leaves. Take the remaining cabbage out of the water and run cold water over the head until you can handle it easily. When cool, chop the head of cabbage into 1/2-inch shreds and put back in hot water to cook until soft (2-3 minutes). Drain & set aside.

Cook bacon in large skillet until crisp. Remove bacon with slotted spoon and set aside. Discard all but 2 tablespoons of bacon drippings. Add onion to skillet and cook over medium heat until tender. Add 3/4 cup cream, sage and cooked, shredded cabbage. Simmer until cream cooks down and thickens, stirring occasionally. Season with salt and pepper to taste. Add all but 2 tablespoons of the cooked bacon.

Preheat oven to 350 degrees. Prepare a shallow casserole dish big enough to hold packets in a single layer. Grease with butter or vegetable spray.

To assemble, take one large cabbage leaf and remove thick center rib, if desired. (I leave it in because it stays a little crispier and I like that.) Spoon about 1/4 cup cabbage/onion mixture into leaf. Enclose mixture in the leaf by folding sides over mixture and rolling to make a small packet. Place packet in prepared pan, seam-side down. Repeat with remaining leaves and mixture. Brush tops with remaining 1/4 cup cream and sprinkle with remaining bacon. Cover with foil and bake 25-30 minutes, or until heated through.

6-8 servings

~

Combine this with a salad and a slice of bread for a light summer meatless supper.

~

Inspiration: I went to visit childhood neighbors of my husband, Helen and Vince McDermott, and this recipe was on their table. I copied it onto a small yellow piece of paper and it's still in my file on the yellow paper.

South of the Border Squash

1½	pounds summer squash, yellow is best but half zucchini is okay too
1	medium onion, chopped (½-1 cup)
2	tablespoons butter
1	(4 ounce) can diced green chilies
2	tablespoons flour
1	teaspoon salt
6	ounces Monterey Jack cheese, shredded (1½ cups)
1	cup small curd cottage cheese, drained
1	egg
2	tablespoons chopped parsley
½	cup grated Romano cheese

Preheat oven to 400 degrees.

If squash is large, cut in half and remove seeds with a spoon or melon baller, especially zucchini squash. Cut squash in ½-inch dice, set aside.

Melt butter in a large skillet over medium-high heat. Add onion and sauté until translucent. Add squash cubes and cook two minutes stirring constantly. Sprinkle with flour then fold in chilies and season with salt.

Place in a greased two-quart baking dish or any dish that allows the squash to be ¾-1-inch thick. Sprinkle with Monterey Jack cheese.

Combine cottage cheese, egg and parsley. Layer over Monterey Jack cheese and sprinkle with Romano cheese. Bake uncovered 25-30 minutes until heated through and lightly brown.

Sweet & Yummy Corn Pudding

This is great for potluck dinners. Although better hot, it works well at room temperature.

10-12 servings

~

* I use home-grown frozen corn, but canned corn works fine.

~

Inspiration: Southern Living

¼	cup sugar
3	tablespoons flour
2	teaspoons baking powder
1	teaspoon salt
6	eggs
2	cups heavy cream
½	cup butter or margarine, melted
4	cups corn*

Preheat oven to 350 degrees.

In a small bowl, combine sugar, flour, baking powder and salt. Set aside.

In a large bowl, beat eggs then add cream and butter. Whisk in dry ingredients until smooth. Add corn and stir. Pour into a greased 9x13-inch baking dish or 10 (5-6-ounce) greased ramekins.

Bake 35-45 minutes or until deep golden brown and mixture is set.

Sweet Potato, Peach & Cashew Bake

I love this dish. I learned to eat sweet potatoes when I made this dish.

6-8 servings

1½   pounds sweet potatoes or yams, about 2 large or 3 medium (I prefer the dark-skin yams)
1   (29-ounce) can peach halves, drained & coarsely chopped
½   cup firmly packed light brown sugar
¼   teaspoon ground ginger
½   teaspoon salt
2   tablespoons cornstarch
3   tablespoons butter
½-1   cup salted cashew halves or pieces

Boil unpeeled potatoes in water, just until you can get a fork through the thickest part (approximately 20-30 minutes). Don't overcook them or they will get mushy during baking. Peel and coarsely chop (about 1-inch cubes).

Preheat oven to 400 degrees.

In a small bowl, combine brown sugar, ginger, salt and cornstarch. Grease casserole dish with butter or vegetable spray. (The best dish to cook this in is a shallow casserole such as a 7x11-inch so that you only have one layer of potatoes and one layer of peaches.) Layer sweet potatoes, sprinkle a little extra salt directly on the sweet potatoes, then layer peaches on top. Top with sugar mixture and dot with butter. Cover and bake for 30 minutes. Uncover and top with cashews. Continue to bake for another 10-15 minutes until bubbly.

I have a problem thickening the juice as it bakes because the peaches release liquid as they cook. I add cornstarch to thicken the sauce. However, in order for the cornstarch to thicken, the dish must get to boiling temperature, and this takes at least 30 minutes, which tends to overcook the sweet potatoes. That is why it is important to undercook the potatoes in the beginning.

If you can find arrowroot you can use that instead of cornstarch. It has a lower thickening temperature and makes a lovely clear sauce.

Julienne Potatoes

French fry shape but you bake them.

6 servings

2   pounds potatoes (if you want long julienne strips, get russets, I prefer all-purpose white or Yukon Gold if you can find them)
½   cup butter
1   tablespoon beef base

Preheat oven to 350 degrees.

Peel potatoes, cut in julienne strips about the shape of a french fry and put in a 7x11-inch baking dish. Melt butter and stir in beef base to dissolve. Pour over potatoes and stir to coat. Cover with foil and bake 40-50 minutes, until done, stirring 2-3 times during baking.

If you like onions, try half a (1-ounce) package of dry onion soup in place of the beef base.

Inspiration: Lipton Soup advertisement

Cheesy Potatoes

10-12 servings

~

This recipe holds its heat very well, especially if you make it in a Pyrex dish. Great for picnics and potlucks.

~

*You can also buy the loose, shredded hash browns, but I don't think it tastes quite as good.

~

Inspiration: a Martha Bohlsen recipe, 1973

1/2	cup butter or margarine
2	cups half and half or evaporated milk
10	ounces Velveeta cheese, cut in cubes
10	ounces sharp cheddar cheese, shredded (about 2 1/2 cups)
2	(27-ounce) packages frozen hash brown patties*

Preheat oven to 350 degrees.

In a medium saucepan, melt butter or margarine. Add half and half and heat gently over medium heat. When warm, add Velveeta. Heat and stir until melted then add cheddar cheese and stir to melt.

Put 8 frozen patties on the bottom of a greased 9x13-inch baking dish. Pour about 1/3 of the cheese sauce over the patties. Slightly thaw remaining patties (use your microwave) and separate the patties to cover the top of the first layer. Pour remaining sauce over the top layer of potatoes.

Bake, uncovered, for 50-60 minutes, until lightly brown. Let rest 5-10 minutes to set up if you want to cut into serving pieces.

Diced Potatoes with Bacon Cream

How could this be bad — potatoes, onions, cream and bacon!

4-5 servings

~

If you want to use less cream, try using 1 cup cream, but thicken it with 2 tablespoons cornstarch plus 2 tablespoons water, until you get the desired consistency.

~

If you like the German potato salad flavor, add 1-2 tablespoons of cider vinegar to the onions before you add the cream. I like that too.

~

Inspiration: *Bon Appétit*, 1999

2	tablespoons oil or butter
1 1/2	cups chopped onion, divided
3	garlic cloves, minced
6	cups diced (1/2-inch) potatoes (I like Yukon Gold or all-purpose white)
	beef broth to cover potatoes (1 1/2-2 cups)
1/2	pound bacon
1 1/2	cups heavy cream

In a large frying pan, heat 2 tablespoons oil or butter and sauté 1 cup onion until soft, about 2 minutes. Add garlic and cook, stirring constantly, about 1 minute. Add potatoes and enough broth just to cover potatoes. Reduce heat and cook gently until potatoes are soft, 10-15 minutes, stirring occasionally. The water should be just about all absorbed or evaporated when potatoes are done. If necessary, drain off excess broth or thicken the broth with a mixture of equal parts cornstarch and water.

While potatoes are cooking, make the sauce: Cut bacon into small pieces — either across the slices to dice or lengthwise for julienne. Fry until crisp. Drain, reserving 2 tablespoons of drippings, and set aside. Using reserved drippings, sauté 1/2 cup onion in a medium saucepan until soft. Add cream and cook gently until reduced by about half. Add bacon and serve with or over potatoes. Sauce can be made ahead and reheated. Cream overflows very easily when cooking, so be careful.

Oven Roasted Potatoes

Simple & good. A great combination. Pictured on page 89.

Pictured on page 89.

4-5   large potatoes (my favorite for this recipe are the white all-purpose but russets work)
1/2   cup butter, melted (no substitutes)
        seasoned salt

Preheat oven to 400 degrees.

Peel potatoes, cut into large chunks (1-1 1/2-inch) and place in a large bowl. Try to make them all about the same size so they cook evenly. Cover with melted butter and place on baking pan that is just big enough to hold potatoes in a single layer. Sprinkle generously with seasoned salt. Bake 60-70 minutes until potatoes are done and they have crisp edges. It is best to turn them halfway through the baking, but I don't usually take the time and they turn out fine.

6-8 servings

Baking time is variable. If you have a large pan, it can take up to 1 1/2 hours to get the nice crispy edge, so plan ahead. They are easy to reheat or keep warm if they get done before you are ready.

"Parmesan" Potatoes

In case you missed it in my Ramblings in the front of the book, I always use Romano cheese when it says Parmesan.

6   large potatoes
1/4   cup flour
1/2   cup grated Romano or Parmesan cheese
1   teaspoon seasoned salt
2   tablespoons vegetable oil
        vegetable spray

Preheat oven to 400 degrees.

Peel potatoes and cut in large wedge shapes. Mix flour, cheese and seasoned salt in a plastic bag. Moisten potatoes with water and put in the plastic bag, a few at a time. Shake to coat.

Pour vegetable oil on a baking sheet. (If you have parchment paper, use it for this recipe to help keep the potatoes from sticking — pour the oil right on the parchment.) Place potatoes on baking sheet and spray potatoes with cooking spray. Bake 50-60 minutes, turning once during baking.

6 servings

Inspiration: *Iowa Farmer Today*, 1994

Twice-Baked Potatoes

This seems like a lot of work for something quite easy. Don't be afraid to try. If you make these ahead — and it's great to do even 1-2 days ahead — plan on 1 hour to reheat them.

I needed a quick reference to make anywhere from 6-50 potatoes, so I settled on this formula. I don't think these are the last word in twice-baked potatoes, but it's a starting point for you.

For each serving-size baking potato (not those monster bakers)

1	ounce cream cheese
2	tablespoons butter or margarine
	salt to taste
	enough milk to make the right consistency
	shredded cheddar cheese for topping

Thoroughly wash potatoes, prick with a fork in several places and bake in a 400-degree oven for 1 hour, until soft when squeezed.

As soon as potatoes are cool enough to handle, cut a small slice off the top of the long side and remove the pulp, trying not to break the shell. Reserve the shell. Rice or mash pulp and beat in cream cheese, butter, salt and enough milk to make the consistency you like. If the potatoes are hot enough, they will melt the butter and cream cheese. I have also found that if the potato pulp is cold, you may add more milk than you need — then the potatoes will be too soft when they are baked. Check for seasoning and spoon into potato shells. (I use a pastry tube without a tip to pipe the potatoes into the shells — it's very fast this way.)

Put potatoes in a greased baking pan, cover with foil and bake at 400 degrees for 30-40 minutes, until heated through. Uncover, sprinkle with cheddar cheese and put back in the oven for 3-4 minutes, to melt cheese.

Desserts

Graham Cracker Crust

$1\frac{1}{2}$	cups crushed graham crackers*
2	tablespoons sugar
6	tablespoons butter or margarine, melted

If you have a food processor, you can do everything in it. Crush graham crackers to fine crumbs. Add sugar & butter.

If you don't have a processor, crush crackers in a plastic bag using a rolling pin. Combine crumbs, sugar and butter in a bowl. Mix well.

Press crumb mixture into a 9-inch layer cake pan, pie plate or spring form pan, pressing $1\frac{1}{2}$ inches up the sides.

Chill until filling is ready or bake at 350 degrees for 8 minutes, just until slightly brown, to set the crust.

*I use Nabisco Honey Maid Graham Crackers. One rectangular package of 22 squares makes about $1\frac{1}{2}$ cups crushed crackers.

Basic Pie Crust

For 9-10-inch pie or tart shell

1	egg yolk
$\frac{1}{2}$	cup ice water
1	cup plus 2 tablespoons flour
$\frac{1}{2}$	teaspoon salt
1	teaspoon sugar, if making crust for a sweet filling
$\frac{1}{4}$	cup butter
$\frac{1}{4}$	cup solid vegetable shortening

This recipe gives ingredients and general directions for making a pie crust. For those who have never made a crust before, detailed directions can be found in a general cookbook, which will probably have wonderful pictures to help you. I use a food processor to make the dough. If you would like to use a food processor, refer to your manual for specific directions.

Combine egg yolk and ice water. (This will be enough for two or three crusts, so you can cover and save the remaining in the refrigerator for one or two days.) Cut the butter & shortening into the dry ingredients. Sprinkle water/egg yolk mixture, one tablespoon at a time, onto the butter mixture, until all flour is moistened. Gather into a ball. Flatten ball into a disk and roll out to fit your pie plate. Carefully place the dough into the pie plate, crimping the edges.

When baking the shell without filling, chill in the freezer about 20 minutes before baking. To keep the crust from puffing up during baking, press a large piece of aluminum foil onto the chilled crust. The foil should be big enough to cover the top edge of crust. This helps keep the top edge from over browning, especially when partially baking a crust. Fill the aluminum foil with dry beans or rice to cover the bottom of the pie shell. Bake at 425 degrees for 8-12 minutes, then remove foil weight and bake 3-4 minutes more until lightly brown. If you are partially baking the crust, it doesn't need to have as much browning because it will get baked again.

This dough recipe is very rich (i.e. a high ratio of fat to flour), but I like it that way. It sometimes falls apart when I roll and place it in the plate, but I just press it back together and patch the holes.

I have never found that pricking a crust to let air escape works for me. The air might escape, but the filling runs through those holes, especially if it is a partially baked shell with a quiche filling.

Chocolate Hazelnut Torte

Pictured on page 93.

3/4	cup butter
3	ounces unsweetened baking chocolate (I use Hershey's)
1 1/2	cups firmly packed light brown sugar
3	eggs
1	teaspoon vanilla
1	cup all-purpose flour
1/2	teaspoon salt
1/2	cup coarsely chopped hazelnuts
6	ounces white baking chocolate
1	tablespoon solid vegetable shortening
2	tablespoons semi-sweet chocolate chips
1/2	teaspoon solid vegetable shortening

Preheat oven to 350 degrees. Grease an 8-inch round cake pan.

In large saucepan, melt butter and unsweetened chocolate over medium heat, stirring constantly. When melted, remove from heat and stir in brown sugar. Add eggs and vanilla. Lightly beat mixture by hand just until blended. (Do not overbeat or torte will rise during baking then fall and crack.) Stir in flour and salt. Pour mixture into prepared pan. Sprinkle with nuts. Bake 20-25 minutes. You will know it is done if the middle of the torte starts to rise higher than the edge. It should shake just a little in the middle when done.

Cool then refrigerate. It should be very cold to remove from pan easily. To remove from pan, run a knife around the edge of the torte and warm the bottom of the pan just a little over a burner. Then flip the torte out onto your hand or a plate and quickly flip it back onto a serving platter with nut side up.

Topping: In heavy saucepan (or microwave), melt white chocolate and 1 tablespoon shortening, stirring constantly. When melted, pour over top of torte, spreading as needed to cover, letting some drizzle over the edge. In the same saucepan, melt chocolate chips and 1/2 teaspoon shortening. Drizzle over top of white chocolate in horizontal lines. Then run a knife or spatula through the chocolate four or five times, alternating direction to make the design. Chill before serving.

8-10 servings

Hazelnuts are sometimes difficult to find. Slivered almonds will work as well.

The best way to cut this is to freeze completely. Remove from freezer, wait 15-20 minutes and cut with a heavy knife. You can make very thin slices this way.

If you cut this in very small wedges it makes a great finger dessert on a cookie tray. See picture on page 92.

Inspiration: *Better Homes & Gardens*, 1988

Basic Chocolate Cake

This is a very old recipe and it is sometimes called "Wacky Cake." It is a good option when you need an eggless cake.

1½	cups flour
1	cup sugar
3	tablespoons cocoa
1	teaspoon baking soda
¾	teaspoon salt
1	tablespoon vinegar
6	tablespoons vegetable oil
1	cup cold water

Preheat oven to 350 degrees.

In mixer bowl, stir together flour, sugar, cocoa, baking soda and salt. Mix in vinegar, oil and water, blending just until dry ingredients are well moistened. Do not overbeat.

Bake in a greased 9-inch round or 9x9-inch square cake pan 25-35 minutes. Double the recipe for a 9x13-inch pan. If you want a thinner cake, more like a bar, bake a single recipe in a 9x13-inch pan for 15-20 minutes.

Devil's Mousse Cake with Crème de Cacao Cream
Pictured on page 95.

Pictured on page 95.

1   recipe Basic Chocolate Cake (opposite page)
     (this should be baked in a 9x13-inch pan with parchment paper on
     the bottom and up the ends so that you can get it out of the pan for
     easier handling. Cool, then put in freezer before filling.)

Filling
1   cup whipping cream
2   tablespoons sugar
1   teaspoon vanilla
4   ounces semi-sweet baking chocolate or for a sweeter filling, use half milk
     chocolate (such as Symphony candy bar)
1   tablespoon vegetable shortening

Crème de Cacao Cream
1½   cups whipping cream
3   tablespoons sugar
1   teaspoon vanilla
¼-½ cup white Crème de Cacao, to taste

Filling: Whip cream, sugar and vanilla to soft peaks. In microwave-safe bowl, melt chocolate and shortening (1-2 minutes). Stir to combine and fold into whipped cream. The chocolate should be warm to combine well with the cream. I know it's scary to put warm chocolate into cold whipped cream, but it works.

Remove cake from freezer and from pan. Peel off parchment paper. Cut cake lengthwise into 3 even strips of 3x13 inches. Put half the filling on each of two strips and stack them on top of each other. Top with remaining strip. If you are not serving this in front of your guests, it is easier to cut if the filled loaf is on its side. Take a long knife, run it under the cake and carefully turn it onto its side. Cover and refrigerate until time to serve. This recipe is fine made several hours ahead of service.

To serve: Whip 1½ cups whipping cream with 3 tablespoons sugar and 1 teaspoon vanilla just until it <u>begins</u> to thicken. Add Crème de Cacao and stir until blended. Put ¼ cup cream mixture on a serving plate. If desired, decorate the cream with a little commercial chocolate sauce. Then cut a ½-inch slice of cake and put it on top of the cream.

12 servings

Inspiration: I read a general description of a Mississippi Mud Cake in the newspaper one day. This is what I thought it sounded like from the description.

Chocolate Praline Cake

Pictured on page 93.

8-10 servings

Inspiration: *Pillsbury Bake-Off,* 1988

½	cup firmly packed light brown sugar
¼	cup butter
¼	cup heavy cream
1	cup pecan halves, toasted
1½	cups flour
1	cup granulated sugar
3	tablespoons cocoa
1	teaspoon baking soda
¾	teaspoon salt
1	tablespoon white vinegar
6	tablespoons vegetable oil
1	cup cold water

Heat brown sugar, butter and cream in a small saucepan or in the microwave until butter is melted. Pour into a 9-inch round cake pan and sprinkle pecan halves on top. Allow to cool, then freeze. (Freezing this layer helps keep it from bubbling over during baking. If you don't have time to freeze this, it is not crucial.)

Preheat oven to 350 degrees.

In mixing bowl, combine flour, granulated sugar, cocoa, baking soda and salt. Then add vinegar, oil and water and mix until combined. (I mix this by hand with a whisk, but it can be prepared in a mixer. Just mix until no signs of flour remain.) Pour cake mixture in pan on top of caramel layer. To help ensure no boil over, be sure the batter touches the sides of the pan all the way around — no air bubbles. This is not a perfect system — don't say bad words about me when it boils over. It happens to me too.

Bake 35 minutes. Allow to cool completely in the pan. When ready to serve, run a knife around the edge of the cake and heat the pan on top of a stove burner for a few seconds to loosen the caramel. Turn over onto serving plate so the caramel side is up. Serve with sweetened whipped cream, ice cream or just as is.

Warm Chocolate Cake with a Soft Heart
a.k.a. Warm Chocolate Cake with a Warm Fuzzy Tummy*

Pictured on page 92.

6 individual cakes

1/2	cup butter
4	ounces semi-sweet baking chocolate (I use Hershey's)
3	tablespoons flour
2	tablespoons coffee-flavored liqueur (I use Kahlúa)
scant 1/2	teaspoon salt
3	extra large egg yolks
3	extra large egg whites
3	tablespoons sugar
	caramel, chocolate or raspberry sauce (optional)

Preheat oven to 375 degrees.

Spray 6 (5 or 6-ounce) ramekins well with vegetable spray and place on cookie sheet. In a heavy medium saucepan over medium heat, melt butter and chocolate. Remove from heat and cool slightly. Add flour, liqueur, salt and egg yolks. Stir to combine.

In a large mixing bowl, beat egg whites with an electric mixer until soft peaks form. Gradually add sugar and continue to beat until peaks are stiff.

Stir about 1/4 of the egg white mixture into the chocolate mixture. Then fold chocolate mixture into remaining whites. Fill prepared ramekins almost even with the top. Bake 10 minutes until puffed and the edges are firm, but center is still soft. Remove from oven and let rest 2-4 minutes.

If you want to serve with a sauce try the Caramel Sauce (recipe below), commercial chocolate flavored syrup or Raspberry Purée (page 130). Put some sauce on the serving plate and invert the ramekin on top. The cake should slide out easily. Sprinkle with powdered sugar and serve with ice cream.

*One of my customers liked this dessert and would try to order it but could never remember the name quite right, so he came up with his own name with similar parts!

These can be reheated very easily, one at a time, in the microwave for 10-20 seconds or all at once in a low-temperature oven (about 300 degrees) for 10 minutes.

Inspiration: *Sunset*

"Caramel" Sauce

This is an all-purpose brown sugar sauce. It is really more like a butterscotch sauce, but it is what I use when I see "caramel sauce" in most recipes.

2	tablespoons butter
1/4	cup light corn syrup
1/2	cup firmly packed light brown sugar
1/4	cup heavy cream

In a small, heavy saucepan, melt butter. Add corn syrup and brown sugar. Cook over medium heat until mixture boils. Boil about 45 seconds, until foam is a light caramel color. Remove from heat and stir in cream. Cool.

Makes about 3/4 cup

Inspiration: *Joy of Cooking*

Tin Roof Tart

8-9 servings

The chocolate needs to feel very warm to medium hot to blend into the cream. If it is too cool, your mixture will look like chocolate cottage cheese. It will taste okay, but not have the smooth chocolaty look you would like. If it is too hot it will melt the cream. If this happens, put it in the freezer and wait for it to set up. You might ask how I know all this?!

1	9-inch pre-baked tart or pie shell
1½	cups salted Spanish peanuts
1	recipe Caramel Sauce (page 121) or 1 cup commercial caramel topping
1½	cups whipping cream
3	tablespoons sugar
1	teaspoon vanilla
4	ounces semi-sweet baking chocolate (I use Hershey's)
1	tablespoon solid vegetable shortening

Sprinkle peanuts in bottom of baked pie shell. Pour caramel sauce over peanuts in pie shell. Refrigerate to cool and set.

In mixing bowl, combine whipping cream, sugar and vanilla. Beat until soft peaks form. Reserve about 1 cup whipped cream for garnish. In microwave-safe bowl, combine chocolate and shortening. Microwave to melt chocolate, stirring frequently. Fold warm chocolate mixture into whipped cream and pour onto caramel in pie shell.

Garnish with reserved whipped cream. Can be served right away or cover and refrigerate for several hours before serving.

Tin Roof Tart II

This filling has a better texture when the pie is made several hours ahead of time, but it is more involved. I don't usually have the dessert made ahead so I use the whipped cream method (on the opposite page).

8-9 servings

~

Inspiration: *Midwest Living*, 1994

1	9-inch pre-baked tart or pie shell
1½	cups salted Spanish peanuts
1	recipe Caramel Sauce (page 121) or 1 cup commercial caramel topping
1	tablespoon sugar
1	tablespoon cornstarch
¼	teaspoon salt
⅔	cup milk
2	egg yolks, slightly beaten
4	ounces semi-sweet baking chocolate, coarsely chopped (I use Hershey's)
1½	cups whipping cream
3	tablespoons sugar
1	teaspoon vanilla

Sprinkle peanuts in bottom of baked pie shell. Pour caramel over peanuts in pie shell. Refrigerate to cool and set.

In a small, heavy saucepan combine sugar, cornstarch and salt. Stir in milk. Cook and stir over medium high heat until mixture comes to a boil and thickens. Reduce heat to medium and cook about 1 minute more. Stir about half of hot mixture into the egg yolks, to temper the yolks. Return yolk mixture to saucepan and cook another minute. Remove from heat and stir in chocolate until melted. Cool mixture to room temperature — about 45 minutes. In a mixer bowl, beat cream, 3 tablespoons sugar and vanilla until soft peaks form. Remove 1 cup whipped cream for garnish. Take about ⅓ of the remaining cream and beat into cooled chocolate mixture. Then fold into the rest of the cream. Spread on top of caramel layer, cover and refrigerate until set, about 1 hour. Garnish with reserved whipped cream.

Chocolate Crème Brûlée

10 servings

~

Inspiration: *The Spirit of Christmas Book 2, 1988*

This is the first brûlée I tried and it was a hit. So I tried others and was hooked!

1	quart heavy cream (4 cups)
1/2	cup firmly packed light brown sugar
2	tablespoons granulated sugar
3/4	teaspoon salt
8	ounces milk chocolate candy bar, broken into pieces (I use Symphony)
8	egg yolks
1	teaspoon vanilla
1/2	cup firmly packed light brown sugar
	sweetened whipped cream to garnish, if desired

Preheat oven to 300 degrees.

In a heavy saucepan over medium heat, stir together cream, brown sugar, granulated sugar and salt and heat just to boiling. Add chocolate and remove from heat. Stir until chocolate is melted.

In medium mixing bowl, whisk together egg yolks and vanilla until blended. Whisk about 1/4 of the chocolate mixture into the eggs, to temper the eggs. Pour in remaining chocolate mixture and whisk until blended. Pour mixture through a fine strainer and divide among 10 (5-ounce) greased custard cups or ramekins. Place cups in a larger baking pan. Add enough hot water to the larger pan to come halfway up the side of the cups. Bake 45-60 minutes or until just set — it should shake like gelatin. Remove pan from oven, take cups out of hot water and cool to room temperature. When cool, cover with plastic wrap and refrigerate until very cold, 8-9 hours or overnight.

The problem with covering this dish with plastic wrap is that you run the risk of condensation on the top if it is not cool enough. If you are going to serve this the same day, just refrigerate it uncovered. You don't want condensation on the top because it is nearly impossible to get the sugar to caramelize.

To serve, set oven to broil. Pat top of desserts with a paper towel to remove excess moisture if necessary. Cover the top of each custard cup evenly with a thin layer of brown sugar. Place cups on cookie sheet and broil 4-6 inches from the heat source just until sugar begins to melt. Watch it carefully, the sugar will melt quickly. This caramelizing can be done 3-4 hours before serving. Serve chilled with sweetened whipped cream.

Butterscotch Crème Brûlée

4	cups heavy cream
4	tablespoons butter
¾	cup firmly packed light brown sugar
2	tablespoons granulated sugar
8	egg yolks
¾	teaspoon salt
2	teaspoons vanilla
½	cup firmly packed light brown sugar
	sweetened whipped cream to garnish, if desired

8-10 servings

Inspiration: *Good Housekeeping*, 1994

Preheat oven to 300 degrees.

In a two-quart saucepan, heat cream until tiny bubbles form around the edge of the pan. Remove from heat and set aside.

In a three-quart pan, heat butter and sugars to boiling. Continue boiling 1-2 minutes, stirring constantly. This gives it the caramelized flavor. Gradually whisk in warm cream until mixture is smooth. The mixture bubbles up when you add the cream to sugar, so be careful. Remove from heat.

In medium mixing bowl, whisk together egg yolks, salt and vanilla until blended. Whisk about 1 cup of the hot mixture into the eggs, to temper the eggs. Gradually pour in remaining hot mixture and whisk until blended. Pour mixture through fine sieve.

Pour mixture into 10 greased (5-ounce) individual custard cups or ramekins. Place cups in a larger baking pan. Add enough water to the larger pan to come halfway up the side of the cups. Bake 50-60 minutes or until just set. The center will shake like gelatin. Remove pan from oven, take cups out of hot water and cool to room temperature. When cool, cover with plastic wrap and refrigerate until very cold, 8-9 hours or overnight.

The problem with covering this dish with plastic wrap is that you run the risk of condensation on the top if it is not cool enough. If you are going to serve this the same day, just refrigerate uncovered. You don't want condensation on the top because it is nearly impossible to get the sugar to caramelize.

To serve, set oven to broil. Pat top of desserts with a paper towel to remove excess moisture if necessary. Sprinkle a light layer of brown sugar on each cup. Place cups on a cookie sheet and broil 4-6 inches from heat source just until sugar begins to melt. Watch it carefully, the sugar will melt quickly. This caramelizing can be done 3-4 hours before serving. Serve chilled with sweetened whipped cream.

Raspberry Crème Brûlée

6 servings

~

Inspiration: *Southern Living*, 1995

½	cup granulated sugar
2	cups heavy cream
6	egg yolks
½	teaspoon salt
2	tablespoons raspberry liqueur
1	teaspoon vanilla
1-1½	cups individually frozen raspberries
½	cup firmly packed light brown sugar
	sweetened whipped cream to garnish, if desired

Preheat oven to 300 degrees.

In a medium bowl, combine granulated sugar, cream, egg yolks, salt and liqueur. When sugar is dissolved and egg yolks are mixed, add vanilla. Pour mixture through a fine sieve.

Grease 6 individual custard cups or ramekins. Put 8-10 raspberries in the bottom of each cup. Pour custard on top to fill each cup.

Place cups in a larger baking pan. Add enough hot water to the larger pan to come halfway up the sides of the cups. Bake 50-60 minutes or until just set. The center will shake like gelatin. Remove pan from oven, take cups out of hot water and cool to room temperature. When cool, cover with plastic wrap and refrigerate until very cold, 8-9 hours or overnight.

The problem with covering this dish with plastic wrap is that you run the risk of condensation on the top if it is not cool enough. If you are going to serve this the same day, just refrigerate it uncovered. You don't want condensation on the top because it is nearly impossible to get the sugar to caramelize.

To serve, set oven to broil. Pat top of desserts with a paper towel to remove excess moisture if necessary. Sprinkle a light layer of brown sugar on each cup. Place cups on a cookie sheet and broil 4-6 inches from heat source just until sugar begins to melt. Watch it carefully, the sugar will melt quickly. This caramelizing can be done 3-4 hours before serving. Serve chilled with sweetened whipped cream.

Crème Caramel

I love this dessert. The only thing wrong is that it only takes about five bites and it is gone!

⅓	cup sugar
3	eggs
2	egg yolks
¼	cup sugar
½	teaspoon salt
2	cups half and half
1	teaspoon vanilla
3-4	grates of nutmeg, or ⅛ teaspoon ground

Source: a good friend, Charlotte Smith, introduced me to Crème Caramel. This is a variation of her recipe.

Preheat oven to 300 degrees. Grease 6 (5-ounce) custard cups or ramekins.

In a small, heavy saucepan over medium heat, melt ⅓ cup sugar until golden brown. Do not stir until it begins to melt. The sugar should be a rich caramel color. I like a medium-dark caramel, but some people like it a little darker. When it reaches the desired color, quickly divide among prepared ramekins. It will harden when it hits the dish and that is okay. Just distribute the sugar as best you can. You can always go back and put more in each cup.

In a medium bowl, combine remaining ingredients (eggs - nutmeg) and stir to dissolve sugar. Pour mixture through a fine sieve then divide evenly among cups. Place cups in a large pan. Add enough hot water to the larger pan to come halfway up the sides of the cups. Cover with foil and bake for about an hour. Watch carefully and don't overcook. The custard should be just set and still jiggle a little in the center. Remove pan from oven and take cups out of water. Cover with plastic wrap and refrigerate for several hours (6-8) to chill well.

To serve, run a small knife around the edge of each cup and turn out onto serving plates, letting the caramel sauce run down the sides of the dessert.

Cheesecake Basics

The cheesecakes in this book all have similar elements. So I thought I would put the basics all in one place and you can use this information with each cheesecake recipe.

Crust

1½	cups crushed graham crackers
2	tablespoons sugar
6	tablespoons butter or margarine, melted

Mix all ingredients in a food processor or bowl. Press into desired pan. You can use a 9-inch springform pan, a 9-inch round layer cake pan or, if you are lucky to have one, a 9-inch removable bottom round cake pan.

Press crumbs onto the bottom and 1-1½ inches up the sides of the pan. It is not necessary to prebake. However, if you plan to freeze all or part of your cheesecake, press crumbs on the bottom only and prebake it at 350 degrees for 8-10 minutes — it helps the crust from getting too soggy when thawed.

Baking

I have seen many methods of baking cheesecakes. From using a water bath to very high heat for a short time. I've found a slow, low-heat method works best for me. Bake at 300 degrees until the cheesecake is set, but still shakes a little like gelatin. If the cheesecake doesn't have a sour cream topping, I turn the oven off, leaving the cheesecake inside for another 30-40 minutes to cool very slowly. After removing cheesecake from oven, run a knife around the edge to help prevent cracking when cooled.

Removing

If you have a springform pan, you have no problem. However, if you bake it in a round layer cake pan, you can "unmold" if you will, the cheesecake by running a knife around the edge of a well chilled cheesecake, then gently heat the bottom over a burner for 30-60 seconds. Place a plate on top of the cheesecake, flip the cheesecake out onto the plate, then quickly flip it back onto a serving plate so that it is right side up. This works only with cheesecake that doesn't have a sour cream topping.

Sour Cream Cheesecake

Charlotte Smith, a friend of mine, introduced me to cheesecake. This is my variation of her recipe. Pictured on page 94.

1	9-inch graham cracker crust (opposite page)
16	ounces cream cheese
3/4	cup sugar
1/2	teaspoon salt
2	teaspoons vanilla
2	tablespoons fresh lemon juice
4	eggs
1 1/2	cups sour cream
2	tablespoons sugar
1	teaspoon vanilla

Preheat oven to 300 degrees.

In a mixer or food processor, combine cream cheese and 3/4 cup sugar. Beat or process until very smooth. Mix in salt, vanilla and lemon juice. If using a mixer, add eggs, one at a time, beating after each addition. If using a food processor, add all eggs at once and process to combine. Pour into prepared pan and bake in middle of the oven 40-50 minutes, just until set. It should jiggle a little like gelatin when moved. Remove from oven and increase temperature to 400 degrees.

For topping, combine sour cream, 2 tablespoons sugar and vanilla in a small bowl. Carefully drop by spoonfuls on cheesecake. Spread evenly over top. Return to oven for 3-5 minutes to set sour cream. Cool and then refrigerate.

Serve with your favorite topping such as cherries, strawberries or raspberries.

8-10 servings

We didn't have cheesecake when I was growing up so I was very fortunate to be introduced to this great dessert with this recipe. It remains one of my favorites. Years later my mom was at our house and I offered her a choice of desserts, one of which was cheesecake. She said, "I've never been real fond of cheesecake." Now I see why we didn't have it at our house when I was growing up. My children won't be familiar with mocha desserts either!

Creamy Raspberry Swirl Cheesecake

Pictured on page 94.

8-10 servings

Inspiration: *Food and Wine*, 1986

1	9-inch graham cracker crust (page 128)
16	ounces cream cheese, softened
3/4	cup sugar
1	tablespoon cornstarch
1/2	teaspoon salt
1	teaspoon vanilla
2	tablespoons fresh lemon juice
3	eggs
1	cup sour cream
2/3	cup Raspberry Purée (recipe below)

Preheat oven to 300 degrees.

In a mixer or food processor, combine cream cheese and sugar. Beat or process until very smooth. Mix in cornstarch, salt, vanilla and lemon juice. If using a mixer, add eggs, one at a time, beating after each addition. If using a food processor, add all eggs at once and process to combine. Mix or process in sour cream. Pour into prepared pan.

Holding 1/3 cup of the raspberry purée about 12 inches above the pan, pour in circles into the cream cheese. This makes the raspberry sink into the cream cheese. Then bring the other 1/3 cup of the purée closer to the pan and pour in circles on top of the cream cheese. Do not pour any raspberry purée within a 2-inch diameter of the center, it makes the cake too difficult to cut. With a knife, swirl the raspberry into the cream cheese to make a swirl design.

Bake on the lowest rack of the oven for 40-50 minutes or until cake is just set and jiggles like gelatin. It should not be brown on top. Turn the oven off, leaving the cake inside for 30-40 minutes more. Remove from oven and cool completely. Chill well before serving.

Raspberry or Blackberry Purée
aka Raspberry Wonderful Stuff

1 1/2 cups

1	(12-ounce) package frozen raspberries, thawed
3/4	cup powdered sugar

I love raspberries and I use this wonderful purée for many things from desserts to salad dressing to sauce for chicken. It freezes very well, so save every drop.

Combine raspberries and sugar in blender and blend until smooth. Pour into a fine sieve. Using a rubber scraper, press puréed raspberries through sieve to remove seeds. More sugar can be added if a sweeter purée is desired.

Blackberry purée can be made the same way using frozen blackberries.

Blackberry Cheesecake

I like this first because it tastes good but also because of the color. Pictured on page 94.

8-9 servings

1	9-inch graham cracker crust (page 128)
16	ounces cream cheese, softened
¾	cup sugar
1	tablespoon cornstarch
½	teaspoon salt
2	tablespoons fresh lemon juice
3	eggs
½	cup Blackberry Purée (opposite page)
1½	cups sour cream
1	tablespoon sugar
1	teaspoon vanilla

Inspiration: If you've read any of the other cheesecake recipes in this book, they are all basically the same. This one just has the fruit mixed in rather than swirled. I put a sour cream topping on it to give it a layered look.

Preheat oven to 300 degrees.

In a mixer or food processor, combine cream cheese and sugar. Beat or process until very smooth. Mix in cornstarch, salt, and lemon juice. If using a mixer, add eggs, one at a time, beating after each addition. If using a food processor, add all eggs at once and process to combine. Stir in blackberry purée and pour into prepared pan.

Bake on the bottom rack of the oven for 35-40 minutes, until just set and jiggles like gelatin. Turn off the oven, leaving the cheesecake inside for an additional 35-40 minutes. Remove from oven and preheat to 400 degrees.

Combine sour cream, sugar and vanilla in a small bowl. Drop spoonfuls carefully on top of cheesecake then carefully spread to cover top completely. Return to oven and bake 5 minutes more to set the topping. Remove from oven, cool to room temperature and refrigerate.

Chocolate Marble Cheesecake

Pictured on page 94.

8-10 servings

~

The chocolate/cream cheese mixture is fairly thick. To help with this, be sure the chocolate is very warm, even hot, before you add the cream cheese so it doesn't start "setting up" before you pour it into the cheesecake.

~

Inspiration: *The Vernon Company Cookbook*

1	9-inch graham cracker crust (page 128)
16	ounces cream cheese, softened
3/4	cup sugar
2	teaspoons vanilla
1/2	teaspoon salt
3/4	cup sour cream
4	eggs
3 1/2	ounces milk chocolate candy bar, (I use Symphony) broken in pieces
1	tablespoon solid vegetable shortening

Preheat oven to 300 degrees.

In a mixer or food processor, combine cream cheese and sugar. Beat or process until very smooth. Mix in vanilla, salt and sour cream. If using a mixer, add eggs, one at a time, beating after each addition. If using a food processor, add all eggs at once and process to combine. Pour into prepared pan, reserving 3/4 cup.

In a microwave-safe bowl combine chocolate and shortening. Microwave on high about 1 1/2 minutes or until chocolate is melted, stirring a couple times.

Add reserved cream cheese mixture to melted chocolate and mix to combine. Holding the chocolate mixture about 12 inches above the pan, pour about 2/3 of the mixture in circles into the cream cheese. This makes the chocolate sink into the cream cheese. Now bring the chocolate mixture closer to the pan and pour the remaining mixture in circles on top of the cream cheese. With a knife, swirl the chocolate into the cream cheese to make a swirl design.

Bake on the bottom rack of the oven 35-45 minutes, just until set. The cake will jiggle a little like gelatin when done. Turn off oven leaving cheesecake inside 30 minutes more. Remove, cool to room temperature and chill.

Lemon Curd Cheesecake

I put this together to use up some leftover lemon curd that I had. Turned out pretty good if you like lemon. Pictured on page 94.

1	9-inch graham cracker crust (page 128)
16	ounces cream cheese, softened
1/2	cup sugar
1/4	teaspoon salt
3	eggs
3/4	cup sour cream
3/4	cup Lemon Curd (recipe below)

Preheat oven to 300 degrees.

In a mixer or food processor, combine cream cheese, sugar and salt. Beat or process until very smooth. If using a mixer, add eggs, one at a time, beating after each addition. If using a food processor, add all eggs at once and process to combine. Mix or process in sour cream and lemon curd.

Pour into prepared pan and bake on the bottom rack of the oven for 35-40 minutes, just until set. Turn off the oven, leaving cheesecake inside for another 30 minutes to cool slowly. Remove, cool to room temperature and refrigerate.

8-9 servings

If you like more lemon flavor, add about 1 tablespoon fresh lemon juice.

Lemon Curd

1/2	cup sugar
1/2	cup fresh lemon juice
2	eggs
2	egg yolks
1	teaspoon grated lemon peel (peel from one lemon)
1/2	cup butter, cut into pieces

In a small, heavy saucepan, whisk together all ingredients except butter. Stir constantly over medium-low heat until mixture thickens and leaves a path on the back of a spoon when a finger is drawn across (about seven minutes). Do not boil. Pour into bowl and add butter. Whisk until smooth. Cover with plastic wrap touching the surface of the curd. Refrigerate until completely cool.

Makes 1 cup

For a very smooth curd, combine all ingredients except peel and butter. Cook as directed then pour mixture into a fine mesh sieve. Push it through the sieve with a rubber scraper. Then add lemon peel and butter.

Inspiration: *Bon Appétit*, 1991

Meringue Pie Shell

This is very easy to make with a free-standing mixer, but it can be done with a hand-held mixer with muscles and time.

Inspiration: My mom made Lemon Angel Pie when I was growing up. The other fillings were just extensions that sounded good to me.

3	egg whites
1	teaspoon white vinegar
1/4	teaspoon salt
1	teaspoon vanilla
1/2	teaspoon baking powder
1	cup sugar

Preheat oven to 275 degrees.

In mixing bowl, combine all ingredients except sugar. Whip until soft peaks form. Gradually add sugar and whip until stiff and glossy. Spread in a greased 9 or 10-inch pie plate. Bake in the lower third of your oven for 40 minutes. Cool.

White Chocolate Strawberry Filling for Meringue Pie Shell

Pictured on page 95.

6-8 servings

The filled meringue shell tends to get watery after 4-6 hours, but it will still taste fine.

1	9 or 10-inch meringue pie shell
1	cup whipping cream
2	tablespoons sugar
1	teaspoon vanilla
2-4	cups chopped strawberries
1	cup coarsely chopped white chocolate or almond bark

Whip cream with sugar and vanilla. Fold in strawberries and white chocolate. Spread over meringue shell. Garnish with strawberries if desired. You can serve this immediately or cover and refrigerate.

I have used all types of white chocolate: white chocolate chips, almond bark, summer coating. I even got some high quality chocolate from a local candy shop. They are all fine for this recipe, just find the kind that you like best.

Lemon Filling for Meringue Pie Shell

Pictured on page 95.

6-8 servings

1	9 or 10-inch meringue pie shell
4	egg yolks
	grated peel from one lemon (about 1 teaspoon)
½	cup fresh lemon juice
½	cup sugar
1	cup whipping cream, whipped

In mixer bowl, beat egg yolks until thick and lemon-colored (about 5 minutes). Add sugar and beat well. Mix in lemon juice and rind. Pour into double boiler or small, heavy saucepan and cook, stirring constantly, until thick. Pour into a bowl, cover with plastic wrap touching the custard and refrigerate 1-2 hours to chill.

Fold whipped cream into cooled lemon mixture. Pour into prepared meringue shell. Cover and refrigerate. This needs to chill 4-6 hours if you want nice slices — it takes that long to set up. You might ask how I know this?!

Chocolate Toffee Filling for Meringue Pie Shell

Pictured on page 95.

6-8 servings

1	9 or 10-inch meringue pie shell
2	cups whipping cream, divided
2	tablespoons cocoa
4	tablespoons sugar, divided
2	teaspoons vanilla, divided
4	(1.4-ounce) Skor or Heath candy bars, chopped, divided

Whip 1 cup cream with cocoa, 2 tablespoons sugar and 1 teaspoon vanilla until soft peaks form. Fold in about half the chopped candy. Spread in pie shell.

Whip remaining 1 cup cream with 2 tablespoons sugar and 1 teaspoon vanilla until soft peaks form. Spread on top of chocolate filling. Sprinkle remaining toffee on top. Cover and refrigerate.

Strawberry Cream Pie

8 servings

~

It is important to fold whipped cream into sour cream mixture before you fold in the strawberries. If you don't you will have a mixture the texture of cottage cheese and it will be very hard to fold in the whipped cream. I learned this the hard way!

~

Inspiration: I developed this recipe from two ideas. First the dipping strawberries in sour cream/brown sugar trick and then the pecan cream pie that I like so well.

1	9 or 10-inch baked pie shell
1/4	cup plus 2 tablespoons cold water
1	envelope plus 1 teaspoon unflavored gelatin
1	cup sour cream
3/4	cup firmly packed light brown sugar
1/2	cup granulated sugar
1/2	teaspoon salt
1	teaspoon vanilla
1	cup whipping cream
2	tablespoons granulated sugar
4	cups chopped strawberries

In a small, microwave-safe bowl, combine cold water and gelatin. Microwave on high 30-45 seconds until gelatin dissolves. (You can also do this in a pan on the stove over low heat.)

In a large mixing bowl (not the bowl from your mixer), combine sour cream, brown sugar, 1/2 cup granulated sugar, salt and vanilla. Add the softened gelatin and stir to combine well. Chill until it begins to mound. If most of the ingredients are cold, this happens very quickly, sometimes even before you get it into the refrigerator.

In mixer bowl, whip cream and 2 tablespoons sugar until soft peaks form. Fold into chilled sour cream mixture. Then fold strawberries into cream mixture.

Pour into prepared pie shell. This fills a 9-inch pie shell very full. You might have to fill as much as you can, chill to set, then carefully add the remainder to the top. (Don't refrigerate the remainder or it will be too stiff to pile on top.) Cover and refrigerate at least 2 hours to set. Garnish with sweetened whipped cream and strawberries, if desired.

Pecan Cream Pie

This is a wonderful pie, but the name doesn't really tell the whole story. It should be "Light and Fluffy Pecan Temptation!" Pictured on page 94.

1	9 or 10-inch baked pie shell
3/4	cup firmly packed light brown sugar
1	envelope unflavored gelatin
1/2	teaspoon salt
1	cup sour cream
4	tablespoons butter
4	egg yolks
1	teaspoon vanilla
4	egg whites
1/2	cup granulated sugar
1 1/2	cups toasted pecans, chopped, divided
1	cup whipping cream
2	tablespoons granulated sugar
1	teaspoon vanilla

In a heavy saucepan, mix brown sugar and gelatin. Then add salt, sour cream, butter and egg yolks. Stir over medium heat until mixture thickens slightly and coats the back of a metal spoon. Remove from heat and stir in vanilla*. Pour into a bowl and cool in an ice water bath, stirring frequently. When mixture begins to thicken, and is the consistency of egg whites, remove from cold water bath.

In a mixer bowl, beat egg whites to soft peaks. Gradually add sugar and beat until stiff and glossy. Stir about 1 cup of the egg whites into the custard, then fold in remaining whites. Fold in 1 cup pecans and spoon into crust. Cover and refrigerate until custard is set, about 30 minutes. Beat whipping cream with 2 tablespoons sugar and 1 teaspoon vanilla until soft peaks form. Mound onto pie and sprinkle with remaining pecans.

8 servings

~

Be sure you mix the sugar and gelatin first, then add sour cream, then egg yolks. One time I put the egg yolks right in with the gelatin and I never did get the gelatin dissolved. It was coated with hard cooked egg yolk!

~

* If you have a fine-mesh strainer, pour hot mixture through it into a bowl, pressing mixture through with a rubber scraper. It makes a very smooth mixture. This step isn't mandatory, because I've made this several times without doing it.

~

Inspiration: I found the base for this recipe in *Bon Appétit* in 1984. Since then, I have seen variations of the recipe in many places.

Pumpkin Layer Pie

~

This can also be made in an 8 or 9-inch square pan or doubled and made in a 9x13-inch pan. When using these pans, just press the crust into the bottom.

~

Inspiration: *Better Homes & Gardens,* 1973

1	9-inch baked crumb crust (page 116) using $1/2$ graham cracker crumbs and $1/2$ gingersnap crumbs
1	envelope unflavored gelatin
$1/2$	cup sugar
$1/2$	teaspoon salt
1	teaspoon cinnamon
$1/2$	teaspoon ground ginger
$1/4$	teaspoon ground cloves
$1/2$	cup milk
3	egg yolks
1	cup canned pumpkin (I use half of a 15-ounce can. It might be a little less than one cup, but it works fine and then you can get two pies out of one can.)
3	egg whites
$1/4$	cup sugar
1	cup whipping cream
2	tablespoons sugar
1	teaspoon vanilla
$1/4$	teaspoon cinnamon

In a saucepan, combine gelatin, $1/2$ cup sugar, salt, spices, milk, egg yolks and pumpkin. Cook and stir over medium heat until mixture just comes to a boil and gelatin dissolves. Be careful, this mixture spits at you when it boils. Remove from heat and pour into a bowl (preferably stainless steel, to speed cooling). Place bowl in an ice water bath to cool, stirring occasionally until mixture begins to mound (15-30 minutes).

In mixer bowl, beat egg whites until soft peaks form. Gradually add $1/4$ cup sugar and continue to beat to stiff, glossy peaks. Fold egg whites into pumpkin mixture.

Whip cream, 2 tablespoons sugar, vanilla and $1/4$ teaspoon cinnamon to soft peaks.

Pour half of pumpkin mixture into prepared crust. Top with about $3/4$ of whipped cream mixture. Then carefully spread remaining pumpkin mixture on top of whipped cream. Cover loosely with plastic wrap and chill until firm (1-2 hours). Refrigerate remaining whipped cream mixture to use as garnish for serving.

Lemon Layer Pie

This is my husband's favorite lemon dessert.

	pastry for 2 pie crusts (page 116)
$3/4$	cup sugar
1	envelope unflavored gelatin
$1/2$	teaspoon salt
1	cup water
3	eggs, beaten
$1/2$	cup fresh lemon juice
	grated peel from one lemon (about 1 teaspoon)
2	tablespoons butter
$1^{1/2}$	cups whipping cream
3	tablespoons sugar
1	teaspoon vanilla

Serves 8

~

* If you have a fine sieve, pour hot mixture through it into a stainless steel bowl. A metal bowl is much better to cool this over ice.

~

Inspiration: This is from *Better Homes & Gardens* but it is so old, the date has faded from my recipe.

Preheat the oven to 425 degrees.

Roll half of pie crust pastry to $1/8$-inch thickness, press into a 9-inch pie plate and crimp edges. Chill in the freezer for 30 minutes. Line with foil filled with dry beans or rice and bake 15-17 minutes. Remove foil liner and continue baking 2-3 minutes more, until lightly brown.

Divide remaining pastry in half. Roll each half to $1/8$-inch thickness. Trim one to a $7^{3/4}$-inch circle, the other to an $8^{1/2}$-inch circle. Place on cookie sheet. Prick each pastry round with a fork. Chill in the freezer 30 minutes. Bake 6-8 minutes, until lightly brown. Cool. At this point, you have basically made a pre-baked pie shell and 2 flat pastry rounds.

In medium saucepan, blend sugar, gelatin and salt. Add water and eggs. Heat over medium heat, stirring constantly, until mixture thickens slightly. You are trying to dissolve the gelatin and cook the eggs slightly, but not too much! Pour into a bowl* and add lemon juice, lemon peel and butter. Stir to melt butter. Chill over an ice water bath until mixture mounds (30-60 minutes).

Whip cream with 3 tablespoons sugar and vanilla. Reserve about 1 cup for garnish and fold remaining whipped cream into cooled lemon mixture. Place 1 cup filling in pie shell, cover with $7^{3/4}$-inch pastry round. Repeat with 1 cup lemon filling and the $8^{1/2}$-inch round. Top with remaining filling. Chill to set (3-4 hours). Garnish with reserved whipped cream.

Classic Bavarian Cream

8 (½ cup) servings

1	envelope unflavored gelatin
¼	cup sugar
½	teaspoon salt
1	cup milk (for a softer mixture, you can add ¼-½ cups more)
2	egg yolks
1	teaspoon vanilla
2	egg whites
¼	cup sugar
1	cup whipping cream

Just before you pour the cream mixture into the cups, you may fold in special ingredients such as ½ cup nuts or 1 cup cooked rice. Don't use converted rice because it hardens when it gets cold.

In a small heavy saucepan (or double boiler) combine gelatin, ¼ cup sugar, and salt. Add milk and egg yolks and whisk gently to break up the yolks and combine with sugar and gelatin. Heat carefully, stirring constantly until mixture thickens slightly and coats the bottom of the pan or the back of a metal spoon. DO NOT BOIL. Immediately pour hot mixture through a fine mesh strainer* into a bowl. Add vanilla. Place bowl over ice water (ice water bath) and stir until cool and just slightly mounding (once this starts to set up, it goes very quickly).

* If you don't have a fine mesh strainer, that is perfectly okay, just omit that step.

In mixing bowl, beat egg whites until soft peaks form. Gradually add ¼ cup sugar and continue beating until stiff peaks form. Stir ¼ of egg white mixture into egg yolk mixture. Then fold in remaining egg white mixture. In a mixer bowl, beat whipping cream to soft peaks and fold into egg mixture.

Spray individual molds or serving dishes with vegetable spray. Pour mixture into cups & chill. You can also use a large, greased 4-cup mold.

Toasted Almond Bavarian with Raspberry Sauce
Pictured on page 95.

This dish has great color and is a light dessert after a heavy dinner. Our son picked this as his "birthday cake" one year.

Prepare Classic Bavarian Cream as above, adding ½ cup toasted, chopped almonds to the mixture before pouring into greased individual cups. Chill.

At serving time, dip the bottom of the mold into warm water for a few seconds and unmold onto serving plate. Drizzle with Raspberry Purée (page 130).

Inspiration: *Better Homes & Gardens,* 1974

140

Chocolate Marble Bavarian Pie

17-20	chocolate sandwich cookies
3	tablespoons margarine or butter, melted
6	ounces milk chocolate candy bar (I use Symphony)
2	tablespoons solid vegetable shortening
1	recipe Classic Bavarian Cream (opposite page)

8 servings

~

Inspiration: *Maida Heatter's Pies & Tarts* cookbook

Preheat oven to 300 degrees.

Crust: Crush chocolate cookies in a food processor or in a plastic bag using a rolling pin. Add margarine and process or stir to combine. Press into 9 or 10-inch pie pan. Bake 5-7 minutes, until set. Cool.

Filling: Melt chocolate and shortening in the microwave, (1-2 minutes) stirring to combine. Allow to cool slightly. Prepare Classic Bavarian Cream (opposite page). Pour cooled chocolate over the Bavarian Cream in a single layer. Fold chocolate lightly into the Bavarian using just 2 or 3 folds. The trick is not to overmix. Pour into prepared crust and chill.

Puff Pastry Pears

I love this dessert — it is easy, looks great and tastes great. Pictured on page 91.

Pictured on page 91.

6 servings

*It's easier to just use a salt shaker to sprinkle the pears with salt rather than measuring out ¼ teaspoon and then trying to sprinkle. Just trust yourself and sprinkle without measuring.

Inspiration: *Bon Appétit*, 1990

½	(17.3-ounce) package frozen puff pastry sheets, thawed (1 sheet)
3	tablespoons butter
4	large ripe pears, peeled, cored and cut into ⅓-inch thick slices (I like Bartlett pears)
¼	teaspoon salt*
2	tablespoons fresh lemon juice
2	tablespoons sugar
1	recipe Caramel sauce (page 121)
	powdered sugar

Preheat oven to 425 degrees.

Unfold pastry sheet. The fold lines make a natural marking to make the pear shapes. Lightly mark a center line horizontally across the fold lines creating six sections of pastry. Using a sharp knife, cut out 6 pear-shaped pieces — I just free hand my pears. Start with the stem and go down each side. Place on a greased or parchment-covered baking sheet and bake on the bottom rack of the oven 15-20 minutes until puffed and golden brown. Cool slightly. Carefully pull apart the pears horizontally to make 2 halves.

In a large sauté pan, melt butter over medium-high heat. Add sliced pears and sprinkle with salt. Cook until pears are just beginning to get tender, stirring occasionally (about 5 minutes). Sprinkle with lemon juice and sugar. Continue to cook until sugar is dissolved and lemon juice is reduced (about 2 minutes). The pears are best with a little bit of brown color around the edges.

To serve, place the bottom half of a puff pastry pear on serving plate. Spoon 4-6 pear slices onto pastry. Top with the other half of puff pastry. Sprinkle with powdered sugar and drizzle with Caramel Sauce. You can use purchased caramel sauce if you like. If you like more sauce put a puddle of sauce on the serving plate before you put the pastry on.

The original recipe used a spoonful of pastry cream on the puff pastry before adding the pears. If you want to try this, you can use my Quick Pastry Cream (page 147).

Strawberry Tart

There is no better way to serve strawberry pie when you have perfectly beautiful, ripe strawberries.

8-10 servings

~

1	9-inch baked tart or pie shell
1	ounce cream cheese
2	tablespoons sugar
½	teaspoon vanilla
6	tablespoons whipping cream
2-3	cups strawberries for tart, 3-4 cups for pie

Glaze*

1	cup sugar
2	tablespoons cornstarch
¼	teaspoon salt
1½	cups water
1	(3-ounce) package raspberry-flavored gelatin
1	teaspoon vanilla
1-2	teaspoons fresh lemon juice

In a mixer bowl, combine cream cheese, 2 tablespoons sugar, and ½ teaspoon vanilla. Beat until cream cheese is smooth. Add cream and continue beating until stiff. Spread in bottom of tart or pie shell.

Glaze: In a small saucepan, mix sugar, cornstarch and salt. Add water and stir. Heat to boiling. Boil about 30 seconds, remove from heat and add gelatin, vanilla and lemon juice (start with 1 teaspoon lemon juice then add more if you like a little more zip). Set aside.

Tart: Clean, stem and halve strawberries. Arrange in a single layer on top of the cream cheese layer in the tart shell. Pour glaze over strawberries and chill.

Pie: Clean and stem strawberries. Chop 1-2 cups of strawberries and slice the rest. Spread chopped strawberries over cream cheese layer in the pie shell. Pour a thin layer of glaze over chopped strawberries. Then arrange a decorative layer of sliced strawberries and pour a layer of glaze over the top. Chill. The chopped strawberries make it easier to slice to make a nice looking serving.

Garnish with sweetened whipped cream, if desired.

* This makes enough glaze for 2-3 tarts or 2 pies. I wrote it this way because you use 1 box of gelatin. If you want to use half a box of gelatin, the rest of the ingredients are easy to halve.

~

The extra glaze can be layered in a glass with strawberries or other fruit for another beautiful dessert.

~

Inspiration: a good friend, Judy Floss

Peach Praline Angel Cake

This is a great dessert when you have a little fruit and need a lot of servings.

1	round angel food cake, commercial or homemade
2	cups whipping cream
4	tablespoons sugar
1	teaspoon vanilla
1	(10-ounce) package toffee bits
4-6	fresh peaches, peeled and chopped (about 5 cups)

Whip cream with sugar and vanilla. Add toffee bits and stir.

Using a long, serrated knife, slice cake horizontally into 3 equal layers. Place bottom layer on a serving plate and spread about $1/4$ of the whipped cream mixture on top. Arrange some of the peaches over whipped cream, pushing them into the cream to secure them a little. Use as many peaches as you can without having them fall out when you place the next layer on top. Repeat the cream and peaches with the next cake slice then place the final cake slice on top.

Spread remaining whipped cream on top and around the sides of the cake. Cover and refrigerate until served. This will hold in the refrigerator for 2-3 hours, but after that the juices from the fruit break down the toffee bits and it gets watery. It will still taste good, it just doesn't look great.

I usually serve this with some sweetened fruit on the side.

Easy Fruit Cobbler

This is a great potluck recipe because you can serve it warm with a little ice cream on top, or at room temperature.

1	(8-ounce) can crushed pineapple, undrained, either sugar added or no sugar added
1	(12-20-ounce) bag frozen fruit (I like peaches)
1	(9-ounce) Jiffy yellow cake mix
3	tablespoons sugar
$1/3$	cup butter or margarine, melted

Preheat oven to 350 degrees.

In a 7x11-inch or 9x9-inch greased cake pan, layer undrained pineapple, fruit of your choice and yellow cake mix. With a spoon, gently move some of the fruit in several places to allow the cake mix to filter down to the bottom – maintaining a nice layer of cake mix on top. Sprinkle sugar over top of cake mix, then drizzle butter or margarine over sugar.

Bake until top is nicely brown. This takes anywhere from 30-60 minutes, depending on the fruit you choose and how cold everything is when you start to bake.

8-10 servings if using a commercial cake, 10-12 if using a homemade cake

~

To make peeling peaches easier, submerge them in boiling water for 10-15 seconds. Remove from boiling water and put into cold water. Peel when cool.

~

You can also use 3-4 cups sliced strawberries in place of the peaches.

~

Inspiration: *Creative Ideas*, 1986

6-8 servings

~

Inspiration: This recipe came from the TV show "Live with Regis and Kathie Lee" in 1999

Cherry Crisp

This is a long time favorite.

Filling

2	cups granulated sugar
1/3	cup cornstarch
1/2	teaspoon salt
3	(14 or 15-ounce) cans red, tart, pitted cherries, undrained
1/4	teaspoon almond flavoring
1	tablespoon fresh lemon juice
2-3	drops red food coloring

Crumb topping

2 1/4	cups flour
1 1/2	cups quick-cooking rolled oats
1 1/2	cups firmly packed light brown sugar
1/2	teaspoon salt
3/4	teaspoon baking soda
1	cup butter or margarine

Preheat oven to 350 degrees.

Filling: In a heavy 3-quart saucepan, combine sugar, cornstarch and salt. Mix to distribute the cornstarch with the sugar. Add cherries, including juice. Stir to dissolve sugar. Heat over medium-high heat until mixture comes to a boil, stirring constantly. Be careful, this will spit at you as it boils. Continue boiling 30-45 seconds more, until mixture thickens and becomes clear. Remove from heat and add almond flavoring, lemon juice and food coloring. Stir and set aside.

Crumb Topping: In the bowl of a food processor or a large mixing bowl, combine all dry ingredients (flour through baking soda). Stir. Cut in the butter or margarine using a pulsing action of the processor or a pastry blender. Pat half of the crumb mixture in the bottom of a greased 9x13-inch pan. Pour cherry filling over crumbs, then top with remaining crumb mixture.

Bake 30-35 minutes, until top is lightly brown and you can see a little bubbling on the sides. Serve warm or at room temperature with ice cream, if desired.

12 servings

If you don't like the almond flavor, try adding 1/8 teaspoon cinnamon. It is a very small amount, but it gives it that mysterious taste you can't quite identify.

Inspiration: *Jasper County Farm Bureau Cookbook*

145

Apricot & Cream Sponge Layer Cake

This dessert is layers of sponge cake, apricot filling and whipped cream with a little bit of apricot brandy for a special punch.

8-10 servings

If you like nuts, you could use either toasted almonds or toasted walnuts in the layers too. Yum!

Inspiration: I know this started out as an idea from *Bon Appétit*, but it's changed so much they would not want to claim it!

1	cup sifted cake flour (sift before measuring!)
1/4	teaspoon salt
1	teaspoon baking powder
2	eggs
1	cup sugar
1/2	cup milk
2	tablespoons butter or margarine
1	teaspoon vanilla
1	recipe Apricot Purée (opposite page)
1 1/4	cups whipping cream
2	tablespoons sugar
1	teaspoon vanilla
3	tablespoons sugar
3	tablespoons hot water
1-2	tablespoons apricot brandy

Preheat oven to 350 degrees. Grease and flour a 9x13-inch pan or cut a piece of parchment paper to fit in the bottom of the pan and spray the paper with cooking spray.

In a small bowl, combine flour, salt and baking powder — set aside. In mixing bowl, beat eggs on high until thick and lemon-colored (about 3 minutes). While this is mixing, put milk and butter in a small pan and heat until butter melts. Keep warm. When eggs are thick, gradually add 1 cup sugar and continue to beat about 3 more minutes. Add flour mixture to eggs and stir just to blend. Stir in milk mixture and vanilla. Blend gently. Pour into prepared pan and bake in center of oven 15-20 minutes, until lightly brown and cake springs back when touched lightly. Cool.

Whip cream with 2 tablespoons sugar and 1 teaspoon vanilla.

To make the syrup, combine 3 tablespoons sugar with 3 tablespoons hot water. Stir to dissolve then add 1-2 tablespoons apricot brandy, to taste. (We aren't much for "whoozie" cake but we like this in small amounts. Try 1 teaspoon almond flavoring in this syrup if you don't have the brandy.)

When ready to assemble, turn cake out onto a powdered sugar-covered towel. Cut in 3 equal pieces, crosswise for a wider cake or lengthwise for a longer cake, but narrower slices. Place one piece of cake on a serving board (it needs to be flat, that's why a board is better than a plate). Sprinkle 1-2 tablespoons of syrup over the cake, then spread with a layer of apricot purée. Top that with a layer of whipped cream 1/4-1/2-inch thick. Repeat with cake, syrup, purée and cream. Put the last slice of cake on top and sprinkle with syrup. You can add another layer of apricot purée or leave it off. Frost cake on all sides with remaining whipped cream. Cover and refrigerate to set and let the syrup even out in the cake (1-2 hours or more). Slice and serve.

Apricot Purée

Concentrated flavor that packs an apricot punch!

6	ounces California dried apricots
1/3	cup firmly packed light brown sugar
1½	cups water

Combine all ingredients in a small saucepan. Bring to a boil, reduce heat to medium and cook 20-25 minutes, until apricots are soft and liquid is reduced to about ½ cup.

Pour into a blender container or food processor and blend until smooth. If necessary, add a little water for easier blending. Store in the refrigerator for up to one month or freeze. The consistency needed might change for different uses. Just add more water for easier spreading.

Makes 1¼ cups

This can be used as filling for the twist Danish on page 70 or cake layers or 2 Oatmeal Shortbread cookies (page 159).

Quick Pastry Cream

1	cup half and half
1	cup whipping cream
1	(3-ounce) package cook and serve vanilla pudding mix
1/4	teaspoon salt
1	teaspoon vanilla

In a medium saucepan, combine half and half, cream, pudding mix and salt. Cook over medium-high heat, stirring constantly, until mixture thickens and comes to a boil. Remove from heat, stir in vanilla and pour into a bowl. Cover with plastic wrap, letting the plastic touch the cream to prevent a film from forming. Chill.

Makes 2 cups

Inspiration: This recipe was an accident. I was making pudding according to the directions but I didn't have any milk, all I had was cream, so I used it and voila very thick pudding! So I tried half and half and whipping cream and it was just about right.

Cream Puff Filling

1	recipe Quick Pastry Cream
1/2	cup whipping cream
1	tablespoon sugar
1/2	teaspoon vanilla

Prepare quick pastry cream and chill. Whip cream with sugar and vanilla. Fold into pastry cream for a rich, great-tasting cream filling.

1 recipe will fill 8 medium cream puffs

Jelly Roll

12-15 servings (8-12)

~

I found that Smuckers light strawberry preserves works really well. It doesn't soak into the cake, so the slices look great.

~

Inspiration: *The Des Moines Register*, 1986

Note: This recipe is for a 12x17-inch pan, also called a ½ sheet cake pan. Numbers in parenthesis are for a regular jelly roll pan (10x15-inch).

4	egg yolks (2)
2	eggs (2)
¾	cup granulated sugar (⅔ cup)
1	cup sifted cake flour (¾ cup)
1	teaspoon baking powder (¾ teaspoon)
½	teaspoon salt (scant ½ teaspoon salt)
2	tablespoons vegetable oil (1 tablespoon plus 1 teaspoon)
2	tablespoons water (2 tablespoons)
1	teaspoon vanilla (1 teaspoon)
	jelly or jam to cover the surface — have at least one cup on hand, but could use more
	powdered sugar

Preheat oven to 375 degrees.

Spray pan with vegetable spray. Line pan with parchment paper or aluminum foil. Spray again. In large mixer bowl, beat yolks and eggs at high speed about five minutes until thick and lemon-colored. Continuing at high speed, gradually beat in sugar until mixture is pale and thick.

In small bowl, combine flour, baking powder and salt. Gently fold into egg mixture and blend thoroughly. In small bowl, combine oil, water and vanilla and fold into batter. Spread batter in prepared pan.

Bake in center of oven about 10 minutes, until cake is springy to the touch. While cake is baking, coat a clean dish towel (not terry cloth) with powdered sugar. You can use a fine mesh sieve to sprinkle the powdered sugar — it will make a nice even coating.

Invert hot cake onto towel. Gently peel off paper or foil. Spread with jelly or jam and roll up tightly. The direction you roll the cake will depend on how thick you want it. Rolling from the short side will produce a large diameter roll which is fine for jelly or jam. However, if you are using ice cream or whipped cream, it is hard to roll from the short side, because the filling squeezes out. If you are going to fill the cake with a cold filling (like ice cream), first roll the unfilled hot cake with the towel inside. Let the cake cool, then unroll carefully. Fill with desired filling and reroll without towel. Some other filling ideas are vanilla or chocolate pie filling, whipped cream with strawberries, lemon curd or ice cream.

Carrot Cake

Everyone has a carrot cake recipe. I like this one because it is so moist.

Cake

3	eggs
¾	cup vegetable oil
¾	cup buttermilk
2	cups sugar
2	teaspoons vanilla
2	cups flour
2	teaspoons baking soda
¾	teaspoon salt
2	teaspoons cinnamon
1	(8-ounce) can crushed pineapple, drained
2	cups grated carrots
½	cup raisins, chopped with 1 tablespoon flour

Buttermilk Glaze

½	cup sugar
¼	teaspoon baking soda
¼	cup buttermilk
¼	cup butter
1	tablespoon light corn syrup
1	teaspoon vanilla

Orange-Cream Cheese Frosting

½	cup butter or margarine, softened
4	ounces cream cheese, softened
1	teaspoon vanilla
3	cups powdered sugar
1	teaspoon orange juice
1	teaspoon grated orange rind
	(you can use 1 tablespoon orange juice concentrate in place of orange juice and rind)

Preheat oven to 350 degrees.

In a mixer bowl, beat eggs. Add oil, buttermilk, sugar and vanilla. Beat to combine. Add flour, baking soda, salt and cinnamon. Stir to moisten. Stir in pineapple, carrots and raisins. Pour into a greased 9x13-inch baking pan or 2 greased 9-inch round cake pans. Bake 35-45 minutes, until set in the middle. Remove from oven and immediately spread with buttermilk glaze. Cool completely then frost with orange-cream cheese frosting.

Buttermilk Glaze: In a medium saucepan (don't use a small pan), combine all ingredients except vanilla. Bring to a boil and cook 3 minutes, stirring often. (The mixture will bubble a lot, that's why you need a medium pan.) Remove from heat — the mixture should be a light caramel color. Stir in vanilla and pour over warm cake.

Orange-Cream Cheese Frosting: Beat together butter and cream cheese until light and fluffy. Add vanilla, powdered sugar, orange juice and orange rind. Beat until smooth. Frost cooled cake.

12-15 servings

~

This cake is good for 3-4 days if kept covered and refrigerated. It also freezes great.

~

Inspiration: *Southern Living*, 1981

Marble Bundt Cake

12-16 servings

When our oldest daughter graduated from high school, she wanted to serve this cake at her reception. Not knowing how many people would come, I made eight cakes along with sandwiches, salads and other sweets. Although we had about 100 people that day, we used just one cake. So let me assure you this freezes very well.

Inspiration: *The Des Moines Register*, 1973

1	cup butter or margarine
2	cups sugar
3	eggs
2	teaspoons vanilla
2¾	cups flour
1	teaspoon baking soda
¾	teaspoon salt
1	cup buttermilk or sour milk (1 tablespoon vinegar plus enough fresh milk to equal 1 cup)
1	cup commercial chocolate-flavored syrup
¼	teaspoon baking soda

Preheat oven to 350 degrees.

Grease and flour a 12-cup Bundt pan. In a mixer bowl, cream butter and sugar until light and fluffy. Blend in eggs and vanilla. In a small bowl, combine flour, 1 teaspoon baking soda and salt. Add flour mixture alternately with buttermilk to sugar mixture. Start and end with flour mixture.

In a medium bowl, combine chocolate syrup and ¼ teaspoon baking soda. Add 2 cups of the cake batter to chocolate and mix. Pour vanilla mixture into prepared pan. Then pour chocolate batter over vanilla batter. DO NOT MIX. Bake 55-65 minutes. Cool 15 minutes then remove from pan. Cool completely. To serve, sift powdered sugar on top or drizzle with a chocolate powdered sugar glaze.

Cream-Filled Cupcakes

30-36 cupcakes

Inspiration: *Mingo Community Cookbook*

Cupcakes

2	cups granulated sugar
2	eggs
1	cup vegetable oil
1	cup buttermilk or sour milk (1 tablespoon vinegar plus enough milk to measure 1 cup)
1/3	cup cocoa
1	teaspoon baking powder
1	teaspoon salt
1	teaspoon vanilla
2 1/2	cups flour
2	teaspoons baking soda
1	cup boiling water

Filling

2/3	cup granulated sugar
1/3	cup milk
2/3	cup solid vegetable shortening
1/2	teaspoon salt
1	teaspoon vanilla
3/4	cup powdered sugar

Frosting

1/2	cup margarine, softened
2	tablespoons cocoa
2	cups powdered sugar
	a little milk to make spreading consistency

Preheat oven to 350 degrees.

Cupcakes: In mixer bowl combine, in order, all cupcake ingredients except baking soda and boiling water. Mix well. In a medium bowl, combine baking soda and boiling water — this causes a bubbling reaction, so be sure your bowl is big enough. Add water mixture to cupcake batter, mixing to combine. Using paper-lined muffin tins, fill baking cups 2/3 full and bake 15-20 minutes or until tops spring back when touched. Cool completely before filling.

Filling: In mixer bowl, cream together all ingredients. Beat at high speed until light and fluffy. Spoon mixture into a pastry bag fitted with a small star tip (I use #18). Insert tip into top center of each cupcake squeezing to insert as much filling as they will hold.

Frosting: Mix all ingredients together and spread on each cupcake. I use a mixer for this because it makes the frosting very fluffy.

Napoleon Creams

I always think of Andrew, a high school friend of our oldest daughter, when I make these. Pictured on page 92.

Pictured on page 92.

Bottom Layer
1/2	cup margarine
1/4	cup granulated sugar
1/4	cup cocoa
1	teaspoon vanilla
1	egg, slightly beaten
1 1/2	cups graham cracker crumbs

Filling*
1/2	cup butter or margarine
3	tablespoons milk
1	(3.4-ounce) package vanilla instant pudding mix
2	cups powdered sugar

Frosting
1	cup semi-sweet chocolate chips
1	tablespoon solid vegetable shortening

Bottom Layer: Combine margarine, sugar, cocoa and vanilla in heavy saucepan. Cook over medium heat until margarine melts. Stir in egg. Continue cooking and stirring until mixture is thick (this doesn't take very long). Remove from heat, stir in crumbs and press into an 8 or 9-inch square pan. Chill.

Filling: Cream margarine well. Add milk, pudding mix and powdered sugar. Beat until fluffy. Spread evenly over bottom layer. Chill until firm.

Frosting: In a small microwave-safe bowl, combine chocolate chips and shortening. Microwave on medium for 1-2 minutes or until chocolate is just melted. Stir until smooth. You can also melt this in a saucepan on the stove. Spread over pudding layer. Chill just until chocolate is easy to cut (5-10 minutes). Cut into small pieces (bite-size squares or two-bite rectangles) and continue to chill until very cold.

Makes 45-60 pieces

*I use half of this filling recipe for a 9-inch square pan, but you can use it all if you like. Half the pudding mix is about 1/3 cup.

Butter will make the filling a little harder than margarine when chilled.

Inspiration: *Farm Journal*, 1969

Cookie Dough Brownies

Brownie Base

3	ounces unsweetened baking chocolate
1	cup butter
1	cup firmly packed light brown sugar
¾	cup granulated sugar
3	eggs
1	teaspoon vanilla
½	teaspoon salt
1½	cups flour
1½	teaspoons baking powder

Filling

½	cup firmly packed light brown sugar
¼	cup granulated sugar
¼	teaspoon salt
½	cup margarine, softened
2	tablespoons milk
1	teaspoon vanilla
1	cup flour

Glaze

1	cup semi-sweet chocolate chips
1	tablespoon solid vegetable shortening

Makes 24-30 bars
(they're rich!)

~

Inspiration: This recipe came from the *Pillsbury Bake-Off*, 1997 magazine. They used a brownie mix for the base, but I hardly ever have mixes in the house, so I used my own. This makes a nice variation on the brownie plate.

Preheat oven to 350 degrees. Grease a 9x13-inch pan.

Brownie: In a large saucepan, melt chocolate and butter. Remove from heat and stir in sugars. Mix well. Beat in eggs and vanilla. Stir in salt, flour and baking powder. Pour into prepared pan and bake 12-18 minutes. Do Not Overbake! Cool.

Filling: In a mixer bowl, combine sugars, salt and margarine. Beat until light and fluffy. Add milk and vanilla, blend well. Mix in flour and spread over cooled brownies.

Glaze: In a small microwave-safe bowl, combine chocolate chips and shortening. Microwave on medium for 1-2 minutes or until chocolate is just melted. Stir until smooth. You can also melt this in a saucepan on the stove. Carefully spoon glaze over filling, spreading to cover. Refrigerate 30 minutes. Cut into bars. Store in the refrigerator.

Peanut Butter Cookies

30-36 cookies

~

If you have burnt sugar flavoring, try $1/2$ teaspoon in the dough for a little added flavor.

~

Inspiration: my mother's recipe

1	cup granulated sugar
1	cup firmly packed light brown sugar
$1/2$	cup solid vegetable shortening
$1/2$	cup margarine, softened
1	cup peanut butter, smooth or chunky
2	eggs
2	cups flour
2	teaspoons baking soda
$1/2$	teaspoon salt

Preheat oven to 350 degrees.

Cream sugars, shortening and margarine. Beat in peanut butter and eggs, then slowly mix in the flour, baking soda and salt. Roll in balls about the size of a walnut, roll in sugar and place on a greased or parchment-covered cookie sheet. Smash with a fork in a cross hatch design. Bake 8-10 minutes.

Molasses Crisps

Our family likes these chewy rather than crisp, so we under cook them a little.

30 cookies

~

It's always a challenge to get these out of the oven at just the right moment. However, we have learned that if that moment goes by, these are good dunking cookies!

~

Inspiration: A co-worker in my early days, Nedra Herr

$1/4$	cup solid vegetable shortening
$1/2$	cup margarine
1	cup sugar
1	egg
$1/4$	cup light or mild, unsulphured molasses
2	cups flour
$1/2$	teaspoon ground cloves
$1/2$	teaspoon ground ginger
1	teaspoon cinnamon
$1^1/2$	teaspoons baking soda
$3/4$	teaspoon salt

Preheat oven to 350 degrees.

In mixer bowl, cream shortening, margarine, and sugar. Add egg and beat well. Stir in molasses and mix until blended. Stir together flour, cloves, ginger, cinnamon, baking soda and salt. Mix into molasses mixture. Chill 20-30 minutes for easier handling, but it's not necessary.

Shape into balls (a small ice cream scoop works well for even-shaped cookies) and roll in sugar. Place on greased or parchment-covered cookie sheet and bake 8-10 minutes. Cool slightly on cookie sheet before transferring to cool.

154

Chocolate Chip Cookies

1	cup solid vegetable shortening
1	cup firmly packed light brown sugar
1/2	cup granulated sugar
1	teaspoon vanilla
2	eggs
1 1/2	cups flour
1	teaspoon salt
1	teaspoon baking soda
2	cups quick-cooking rolled oats
6	ounces semi-sweet chocolate chips

Preheat oven to 350 degrees.

In a mixer bowl, beat shortening, sugars and vanilla until creamy. Add eggs and beat until light and fluffy. In a small bowl, combine flour, salt, baking soda and oats. Gradually beat into sugar mixture. Stir in chocolate chips. Drop by well-rounded teaspoonfuls (or small ice cream scoop) onto greased or parchment-covered baking sheet. Bake 8-10 minutes, until golden brown around the edges and light brown in the center. Cool.

30-32 cookies

I can't make regular chocolate chip cookies so when I tried this recipe, it was the look and taste I always thought chocolate chip cookies should be — a little chewy and cracked on the top. The trick to making them chewy is not to overbake them.

Inspiration: *Iowa Farmer Today*, 1992

Cranberry Toffee Oatmeal Cookies

1	cup butter or margarine (I use half of each)
3/4	cup granulated sugar
3/4	cup firmly packed light brown sugar
1/2	teaspoon salt
1	egg
1	teaspoon vanilla
1 3/4	cups flour
1	teaspoon baking soda
1 1/2	cups quick-cooking rolled oats
1	cup toffee bits (or 1/2 of a 10-ounce package)
1	(6-ounce) package dried sweetened cranberries (Craisins)

Preheat oven to 350 degrees.

In a large mixing bowl, combine butter, sugars and salt until light and fluffy. Add egg and vanilla. Beat until combined. Add flour and baking soda, then oats and stir until all dry ingredients are combined. Stir in toffee bits and cranberries.

Drop by rounded teaspoonfuls (or use a small ice cream scoop) onto a greased or parchment-covered cookie sheet. Bake 10-12 minutes — edges should be golden and centers should be just set when done. Remove from oven and let rest 3-4 minutes before removing from the pan.

30-32 cookies

This has become one of our family's favorite cookies. I got the original recipe from Martha Stewart's television show, but she used dried cherries which are wonderful but out of my price range for cookies. She also added chocolate chips but I thought they weren't necessary. The secret ingredient of toffee bits, however, came from her show.

155

Almond Crescents

I like these cookies because they are very delicate. In fact, if I don't break some when I roll them in the powdered sugar, I don't think they are right. You know, those broken ones taste the best.

2/3	cup slivered almonds
1	cup butter, softened (no substitutes)
1/3	cup granulated sugar
1/4	teaspoon salt
1/4	teaspoon almond extract
1 2/3	cups flour*
	powdered sugar

Grind almonds in a blender or food processor using an on-and-off motion.

Beat together butter, granulated sugar, salt, almond extract and almonds. Mix in flour. Chill until it is easy to work with (1-2 hours).

Preheat oven to 325 degrees.

Roll and shape into crescents and bake 14-16 minutes, until set. Let rest on cookie sheet 2-3 minutes before removing. While still warm, roll cookies in powdered sugar. Roll in powdered sugar again after cookies have cooled.

30-40 cookies

*I use 1 cup all-purpose flour and 2/3 cup cake flour, but they are just fine with all purpose only.

Inspiration: This is my mom's recipe

Buckeyes

Pictured on page 92.

1	pound margarine, softened
28	ounces peanut butter, chunky or smooth
1	teaspoon burnt sugar flavoring
	dash salt
2	pounds powdered sugar
12	ounces semi-sweet chocolate chips
1	ounce paraffin wax (about 1/4 of a bar)
1/2	teaspoon burnt sugar flavoring

In a mixer bowl, combine margarine and peanut butter. Add burnt sugar flavoring and salt. Gradually add powdered sugar until too stiff for the mixer. If necessary, mix in remaining powdered sugar by hand. Roll into small balls. Freeze. (These can stay in the freezer for several days before putting the chocolate coating on.)

In a double boiler, melt chips, wax and 1/2 teaspoon burnt sugar flavoring. Using a toothpick, dip peanut butter balls into chocolate leaving a little bit of peanut butter showing at the top (so it looks like a buckeye). Place on waxed paper and refrigerate or freeze.

9 dozen

You might have trouble finding burnt sugar flavoring. We have a local company in Iowa that specializes in food flavoring. Just omit if not available.

Inspiration: *Kitchen Klatter* magazine, 1977

Eskimo Balls

This is a quick no-bake cookie the kids can make. Pictured on page 92.

3/4	cup margarine, softened
3/4	cup granulated sugar
1	tablespoon water
1/2	teaspoon vanilla
1/8	teaspoon salt
3	tablespoons cocoa
2	cups quick-cooking rolled oats
	powdered sugar

Combine first six ingredients (margarine through cocoa) in order, mixing well. Stir in oats. Shape into small balls, about 1-inch diameter. Roll in powdered sugar and chill.

I found if you refrigerate these uncovered, after about a day they get a little crust on the outside. When you bite into them you get the crusty feel and the soft center. I kind of like them that way.

3 dozen

Inspiration: a friend, Marilyn Matthews, gave me this recipe. It is still easy to find it in my file – on the little piece of white paper with red edging.

Salted Nut Bars

These are even better after being stored in an air-tight container for awhile. Pictured on page 92.

3	cups flour
1 1/2	cups firmly packed light brown sugar
1	teaspoon salt
1	cup butter or margarine, softened
2-3	cups salted mixed nuts
1/2	cup light corn syrup
2	tablespoons butter or margarine
1	tablespoon water
1	cup butterscotch chips

Preheat oven to 350 degrees.

In a mixer bowl, combine flour, brown sugar and salt. Blend in 1 cup butter. The mixture will be crumbly. Press into an ungreased 15x10-inch jelly roll pan. Bake 10-12 minutes. Remove from oven and sprinkle with nuts.

About halfway through the baking time, start the topping. In a small saucepan over high heat, combine corn syrup, 2 tablespoons butter, water and butterscotch chips. Boil two minutes, stirring constantly. Pour mixture over nuts, staying within 1/8-1/4-inch of the sides, of the pan. (If you get the butterscotch mixture too close to the sides it gets crispy when baked. Most of the mixture will spread out to the edges while baking.) Return to oven and bake 10-12 minutes until golden brown and bubbly.

Cool completely before cutting.

3-4 dozen

Inspiration: *Pillsbury Simply from Scratch*, 1978

Scroll Butter Cookies

This is a crisp little addition to any cookie plate. I make them for Christmas.

1	cup butter, chilled (no substitutes)
1½	cups flour
¼	teaspoon salt
½	cup sour cream
	zest from one lemon
	about 1 cup sugar

In a large bowl, cut butter into flour and salt using a pastry blender, until mixture resembles coarse crumbs. Stir in sour cream and lemon zest until well blended. Sometimes hands work best for this. Place on waxed paper and shape into a rough 4-5-inch square. Wrap with plastic wrap and refrigerate 1-2 hours.

Unwrap and cut dough into 4 equal pieces, working with only 1 piece at a time. Refrigerate remaining pieces. Sprinkle 2 tablespoons of sugar on a work surface (counter top or pastry cloth). Coat all sides of the dough with sugar. Roll into a 12x5-inch rectangle, turning dough often to prevent sticking. Sprinkle with a light dusting of sugar. Starting at both the 5-inch sides, roll like a jelly roll toward the center, until they meet (like a scroll). Wrap in waxed paper and repeat with remaining dough, making 4 scrolls in all. Refrigerate again, at least one hour.

Preheat oven to 375 degrees. Line cookie sheet with parchment paper or aluminum foil.

Spread ¼ cup sugar on a piece of waxed paper. Cut each scroll crosswise into generous ¼-inch slices, dip each cut side in sugar and place on baking sheet, 2 inches apart. Bake 12-15 minutes until golden brown around edges. Turn cookies over and bake 5 minutes more.

6 dozen cookies

If you have a food processor, you can process butter, flour and salt until mixture resembles coarse crumbs. Add sour cream and lemon zest and continue processing until mixture forms a ball. Continue with recipe as directed.

Inspiration: *Good Housekeeping,* 1978

Oatmeal Shortbread

This recipe came from my sister, Jan. She made them when we visited her in 1972 in Florida and they were just as good when she had them on our visit in 2000 in California! Pictured on page 92.

1	cup butter, softened (no substitutes)
1/2	cup firmly packed light brown sugar
1	teaspoon vanilla
1	cup flour
1/2	teaspoon baking soda
1/2	teaspoon salt
2	cups quick-cooking rolled oats

Preheat oven to 350 degrees.

In mixer bowl combine butter, brown sugar and vanilla. Mix until well combined and fluffy. Combine flour, baking soda and salt. Add to butter mixture and blend. Add oats and mix until combined.

Using about 1/2 of the dough, roll out on a lightly floured board to about 1/8-inch thickness. Cut out desired shapes and place on ungreased cookie sheet. You can also shape these cookies by rolling into small balls and flattening them with the bottom of a sugar-coated glass. Bake 8-10 minutes. They should be crisp.

30-36, 2-inch cookies

~

One of my favorite ways to eat these cookies is to cut them into very small circles, about 1-1/2 inches, then sandwich them with seedless raspberry jam, Raspberry Purée (page 130) or Apricot Purée (page 147). They just pop into your mouth. For something even more special, drizzle the cookie sandwich with melted white chocolate. It is a wonderful Christmas cookie this way.

Lace Oatmeal Cookies

Pictured on page 94.

1/2	cup sugar
1/4	teaspoon salt
1/2	cup butter, softened (no substitutes)
1/2	teaspoon vanilla
1 1/4	cups quick-cooking rolled oats

Preheat oven to 375 degrees.

In mixer bowl, beat sugar, salt, butter and vanilla until light and fluffy. Stir in oats, mix well. Dough will be crumbly.

Drop by rounded tablespoonfuls* onto greased or parchment-covered cookie sheet. Put only 4-6 cookies on each pan. Press with your fingers to flatten slightly. Bake 8-9 minutes or until brown around the edges. They should be very flat.

Remove from oven and cool just until they can be shaped. If they get too hard before you shape them, put them back into the oven for 30 seconds or so to soften.

While warm, these cookies can be shaped into batons by rolling them around wooden spoon handles. They can also be molded into a tube or a cup by rolling them around a one-inch dowel or draping them over an inverted custard cup. Then fill with whipped cream and use as a dessert topped with fruit. They can also be left flat and decorated with melted chocolate chips or white chocolate or sandwiched together with chocolate.

8-10 large round cookies

~

*You can use smaller spoonfuls for smaller cookies.

~

If you haven't started using parchment paper by now, you will want to for this recipe. I've been telling you to use it all through the book. I love parchment paper!

159

Chocolate Mint Bars

4 dozen 1-inch bars

Inspiration: *Bon Appétit*, 1977

A nutty chocolate mint beauty – great for a Christmas tray. Pictured on page 92.

Brownie

³⁄₄	cup flour
1	cup granulated sugar
¹⁄₂	cup instant cocoa mix (the kind you put in milk)
³⁄₄	cup salt
¹⁄₂	teaspoon baking powder
²⁄₃	cup butter or margarine, softened
2	eggs
1	teaspoon vanilla
1	tablespoon light corn syrup
1	cup coarsely chopped toasted almonds

Mint Frosting

2	cups powdered sugar (add ¹⁄₂ cup sugar if planning to decorate as shown in the picture)
¹⁄₂	cup margarine
1-2	tablespoons milk, to make spreading consistency
1	teaspoon mint extract
2-3	drops green food coloring

Chocolate Glaze

1	square unsweetened chocolate
1	tablespoon solid vegetable shortening

Preheat oven to 350 degrees.

Brownie: In a mixer bowl combine flour, granulated sugar, cocoa mix, salt and baking powder. Add butter, eggs, vanilla and corn syrup, mixing thoroughly. Fold in almonds.

Spread batter in greased 9-inch square baking pan. Bake 20-25 minutes, just until edges are slightly firm and center is almost set. Do not overbake. Cool.

Mint Frosting: In a mixer bowl, beat together powdered sugar and margarine. Add milk, a little at a time to get desired consistency. Mix in mint extract and food coloring and spread very smoothly on brownie layer, reserving ¹⁄₃ cup for decorating, if desired. Chill until very cold. Cut into small bars, but don't remove from pan.

Chocolate Glaze: Heat chocolate and shortening in a small pan or a microwavable bowl. When melted, brush evenly over the top of bars, using a pastry brush. Allow chocolate to set, then recut bars.

If you are going to decorate bars, put reserved frosting in a pastry tube fitted with a small flower tip. Pipe a green wreath on each bar.

Miscellaneous

Popcorn Balls

8-10 balls

1   cup sugar
1/3   cup corn syrup (1/2 dark and 1/2 light, or all light)
1/3   cup water
1/4   cup butter or margarine
3/4   teaspoon salt
3/4   teaspoon vanilla
3   quarts popped popcorn (about 3/4 cup unpopped)

For many years, I directed the youth choir at our church and these were always the treats I gave the kids after Christmas Eve service. Many Christmas Eves were spent making these after we had our family gift opening, in preparation for the late night service.

Inspiration: my aunt Opal Hage

In a heavy saucepan, cook sugar, corn syrup, water, margarine and salt until sugar is dissolved. Continue cooking without stirring until syrup heats to soft-ball stage — 238-240 degrees. Remove from heat and stir in vanilla. Pour over popcorn, stirring to coat.

When the popcorn cools enough to hold, rub a little margarine on your hands and shape into balls, pressing just enough to hold the shape.

Sorbet

Makes 3 cups

Quick & easy — who knew!

1   (15-ounce) can fruit cocktail in heavy syrup, drained
1   (12-ounce) can frozen juice concentrate (any flavor, except lemonade)
1-2   cups ice (the more ice, the harder the sorbet freezes)

When I first started my business, sorbet was "the" thing and I didn't have an ice cream freezer. I needed a way to make a fruit ice easy and fast so I made this work for us.

If you have fresh fruit, just add it for a flavor boost such as peaches with white grape peach concentrate.

Combine all ingredients in order in a blender and blend until smooth. Put in a bowl and freeze.

If you want a smoother sorbet, let mixture freeze then cut in chunks and reblend.

To make lemon sorbet, use a can of pears and 6 ounces of lemonade concentrate. I use pears instead of fruit cocktail to retain the white color and only 6 ounces of lemonade because 12 ounces is too strong.

Crusty Chicken Wings

24	chicken wings (about 3 pounds)
1	(5-ounce) can evaporated milk or ⅔ cup half and half
1	tablespoon deli-style or stone ground mustard
2	cloves garlic, minced
1	cup fine dry bread crumbs
1	teaspoon instant minced onion
1	teaspoon seasoned salt
¼	teaspoon seasoned pepper
1	teaspoon chicken soup base

Preheat oven to 400 degrees.

Trim tips from chicken wings. Divide each wing in half by cutting through the joint. Blend milk, mustard and garlic in a shallow dish. Combine bread crumbs, onion, salt, pepper and soup base in another dish. Dip chicken pieces into milk mixture then crumbs to coat well. If you have time, let the chicken marinate 30 minutes in the milk/garlic mixture to soak up a little more flavor. Place on a greased cookie sheet or jelly roll pan. (If you have parchment paper, use it for this recipe!) Bake 35-45 minutes, until tender and brown.

6-8 servings

~

This is one of my favorite chicken wing recipes because you don't have to turn them during baking.

~

Inspiration: *Family Circle Best Ever Chicken Recipes* cookbook

Cardinal Victory Punch

Very economical and very good.

2	packets of cherry flavored Koolaid (or a flavor of your choice)
2	cups sugar
12	ounces frozen lemonade concentrate
8	cups water
1	cup pineapple juice
2	liters carbonated beverage such as sour mix, 7-Up or gingerale

Mix all ingredients except carbonated beverage and freeze. (I like to freeze this in 5-quart ice cream containers.) Two hours before serving, remove from freezer and let set for about one hour. Pour carbonated beverage over the juice in the container. Chop into a slushy mixture and pour into serving dish.

Makes 1 gallon

~

This wasn't always called "Cardinal Victory Punch"— the name evolved. The mascot for our local high school is the Cardinal. We served this at every graduation party for our children. One of our daughters was also a cheerleader and she would volunteer to bring this punch to sports celebrations. Food is a great memory prompt.

~

Inspiration: Judy Floss, a good friend

Guacamole

Makes 3/4-1 cup

This recipe will probably make a guacamole purest go right through the roof, but this Norwegian mid-westerner likes it!

If you have a small food processor, this whips up in about 2 minutes.

Inspiration: *What to Cook for Company* cookbook

1	ripe avocado, pitted, peeled, and mashed (I prefer Haas avocados)
2-3	drops hot pepper sauce
1	tablespoon finely chopped onion
1-2	teaspoons fresh lemon juice — depending on taste and size of avocado
1	clove garlic, minced
1/2	cup seeded and chopped tomato
	salt to taste
1/4	cup mayonnaise

Combine all ingredients and mix well. If using a food processor, combine all ingredients except tomatoes. Process, then stir in tomatoes by hand.

Guacamole Pie

4-6 servings

This is served as a dip, but you might want to provide plates because it is messy — but very good!

If you want to prepare this ahead, make the avocado mixture, spread it on the plate and cover with plastic wrap. Add the toppings just before serving.

Inspiration: *What to Cook for Company* for the avocado layer and Marilyn Vernon for the combination.

2	ripe avocados
8	ounces cream cheese, softened
1	teaspoon garlic salt
1-2	tablespoons fresh lemon juice
3-4	drops hot pepper sauce (or to taste)
1-2	cups shredded lettuce
1	large tomato, seeded and chopped (not too juicy)
1/2	cup chopped onion, such as Vidalia or red
4-6	ounces cheddar cheese, shredded

Halve avocados lengthwise, remove pit and scoop flesh into a bowl, mixer bowl or food processor. Mash with a fork, mix or process. Add cream cheese, garlic salt, lemon juice and hot pepper sauce. Combine until smooth.

Spread mixture on a serving plate in a circle. Top with lettuce, tomato, onion and cheese.

Ham Salad

This is an alternative to the sweet pickle ham salad.

1/2	pound ground ham (about 2 cups)*
1	teaspoon finely minced onion
3	ounces cream cheese, softened
2	tablespoons mayonnaise
1/8	teaspoon dry mustard

Combine all ingredients and spread on crackers or bread.

Makes 1 1/2 cups

~

* To grind ham, use a food processor or a food mill, if you have one. Some meat markets will also grind ham for you.

~

Inspiration: My sister-in-law, Judy Hage

Radish Butter

I love this and radishes aren't my favorite vegetable.

1/2	cup butter, softened
3	tablespoons minced red radishes, plus slices for garnish
1	tablespoon minced chives or the tops of green onions
2	teaspoons minced parsley
1	teaspoon fresh lemon juice
1/4	teaspoon salt (or to taste)
1/2	teaspoon dried or 2 teaspoons minced fresh dill weed

Combine all ingredients and spread on bread. Top with thin slices of radishes. If you want to make a fancy open face finger sandwich, cut the crust off the bread, spread bread with butter, cut in squares or strips and top with radish slices and fresh dill, if available.

Inspiration: *Gourmet,* 1973

A Brief Background with Emphasis on Brief

If you like to do something, you usually have been doing it for a long time. That's the way it has been for me. I grew up on a farm near Inwood, Iowa in the extreme northwest corner of the state. There was always a lot of cooking to be done, and I would rather do that than work outside, so I helped my mom, Leota Hage, prepare meals and bake. That was one of the best gifts my mom could have given me. She let me cook and bake, no restrictions. The last two summers of high school and a couple summers during college, I worked in a private home, mostly cooking because I wasn't very good at cleaning. I graduated from Iowa State University with a double major in Home Economics Education and Textiles. I met my husband, Laird, at school and married after graduation. We moved to a farm near Newton where we still live and Laird still farms. My first job was in the Research and Development department of the Maytag Company. Although my job was testing the washing and drying equipment, I found time to cook in the test kitchen as much as I could.

After our second child was born, I became a stay-at-home mom. As the children got older, I decided to try a small catering business from our home. With the help of some very good friends in Newton who had me help them with some parties, I started to build a business very slowly. Then one day a group called and wanted me to cater something I didn't want to cater because it required equipment I didn't have. I invited them to come to our house. And that's how the home dining started.

That was the only group that year. They came back the next year along with another group from the same town. Two parties in one year! Slowly we started to build an in-home dining business. We had two more babies, so slowly was fine with me. Today we average parties five nights a week and the lunch business is growing to average three to four times a week. Our first group has come back once a year ever since we started. This year was their twenty-second visit.

It's a great business. I get to cook, experiment and try new things and I get to enjoy the fellowship that comes from combining food and friends. It's hard not to like a business that has a party every night. It's been a great time.

If you would like to talk with me about any of the recipes in this book or the business you can reach me by phone at (641)792-5403 or write me, Julie Trusler, 1463 West 62nd St. North, Newton, IA 50208.

Sources

These are some of the mail order sources that I have found very useful to order some of the ingredients and equipment not readily available in the local market.

King Arthur flour and a great variety of baking needs
> The Baker's Catalogue
> P.O. Box 876
> Norwich, VT 05055-0876
> 1-800-827-6836
> www.BakersCatalogue.com

Parchment paper, candy and cake decorating supplies, etc.
> Sweet Celebrations Inc.
> P.O. Box 39429
> Edina, MN 55439-0426
> 1-800-328-6722
> www.sweetc.com

Pastry cloths and basic baking supplies
> Kitchen Krafts Inc.
> P.O. 442
> Waukon, IA 52172-0442
> 1-800-776-0575
> www.KitchenKrafts.com

Great variety of spices in many different forms. Just fun to read through. Great quality.
> Penzey's Spices
> P.O. Box 933
> W19362 Apollo Dr.
> Muskego, WI 53150
> 1-800-741-7787
> www.penzeys.com

Minor's Soup Base distributor for the home cook.
> Allserv, Inc.
> P.O. Box 21743
> Cleveland, OH 44121-0743
> 1-800-827-8328
> www.allserv.com

Remember the local restaurant supply companies will sell to individuals at the will call window. You might have to buy larger quantities, but you can share with friends and relatives and spread out the cost.

Index

A

Almonds

Almond Crescents, 156
Chocolate Mint Bars, 92, 160
Green Bean & Almond Rice, 79, 90
Romaine, Mandarin Orange & Glazed Almond Salad, 23
Toasted Almond Bavarian with Raspberry Sauce, 95, 140

Almond Crescents, 156

Apricot

Apricot & Cream Sponge Layer Cake, 146
Apricot Purée, 147
Carrots & Apricots, 99

Apricot & Cream Sponge Layer Cake, 146

Apricot Purée, 147

Artichokes

Artichoke Cream Soup, 9
Ham & Chicken Bake with Artichokes, 64
Hearts of Palm Salad, 21
Pasta Salad with Mustard Dressing, 32

Artichoke Cream Soup, 9

B

Baby Carrots with Mustard & Brown Sugar Glaze, 98

Bacon

B.O.O.M. Quiche, 68
Broccoli, Bacon & Raisin Salad, 28
Cauliflower Bacon Salad, 28
Cauliflower, Brie & Bacon Soup, 4
Country French Peas, 104
Creamy Cabbage Packets with Bacon & Onion, 109
Diced Potatoes with Bacon Cream, 112
Egg Casserole, 67
Hearts of Palm Salad, 21
Onion Tart, 16
Pork Tenderloin Tournedos, 44, 90
Snappy Green Beans, 105
Spinach Bacon Salad, 27
Spinach Strudel, 107
Zucchini Bacon Soup, 9

Balsamic Vinegar

Beef Tenderloin with Mustard Balsamic Vinegar Sauce, 38
Beef with Wine Sauce, 39, 89

Barley

Barley Casserole, 80
Five Hour Stew, 40

Barley Casserole, 80

Basic Pie Crust, 116

Basic Chocolate Cake, 118

Beans

Black

Hearts of Palm & Black Bean Salad, 29, 87

Green

Green Bean & Almond Rice, 79, 90
Snappy Green Beans, 105

Beef

Beef Tenderloin with Mustard Balsamic Vinegar Sauce, 38
Beef with Wine Sauce, 39, 89
Cheesy Taco Casserole, 41
Five Hour Stew, 40
Stove Top Casserole, 40
Tex-Italian Pasta Fiesta, 42

Beef Tenderloin with Mustard Balsamic Vinegar Sauce, 38

Beef with Wine Sauce, 39, 89

Beurre Blanc, 12

Blackberry Cheesecake, 94, 131

Blackberry Purée, 130

B.O.O.M. Quiche, 68

Breads

Cinnamon Bread, 72
Cinnamon Twist Danish, 70, 84, 85
Cocktail Buns, 72
Crescent Rolls, 70, 84. 85
Crunchy Bread, 75
Overnight Coffeecake, 71
Pull-Apart Cheese Bread, 75
Rye–Carrot Bread, 74
Sticky Cinnamon Rolls, 72

Broccoli

Broccoli, Bacon & Raisin Salad, 28
Broccoli with Orange Shallot Butter, 103
Creamy Pasta with Ham & Broccoli, 65
Ham, Broccoli & Rice Casserole, 66
Norwegian Stir-Fry Broccoli & Carrots, 102
Peas with Broccoli Medallions, 104
Rainbow of Four Vegetables with Hollandaise Sauce, 101

Broccoli, Bacon & Raisin Salad, 28

Broccoli with Orange Shallot Butter, 103

Brown Rice with Mushrooms, Sour Cream & Jack Cheese, 78

Buckeyes, 92, 156

Butterscotch Crème Brûlée, 125

C

Cabbage

Creamy Cabbage Packets with Bacon & Onion, 109
Red Cabbage Salad, 30
Sauerkraut Salad, 31
Srambled Cabbage, 108
Wilted Cabbage Salad, 31

Cakes

Apricot & Cream Sponge Layer Cake, 146
Basic Chocolate Cake, 118
Carrot Cake, 149

Chocolate Praline Cake, 93, 120
Cream-Filled Cupcakes, 151
Devil's Mousse Cake with Crème de Cacao Cream, 95, 119
Jelly Roll, 148
Marble Bundt Cake, 150
Peach Praline Angel Cake, 144
Warm Chocolate Cake with a Soft Heart, 92, 121

"Caramel" Sauce, 121

Cardinal Victory Punch, 163

Carrots

Baby Carrots with Mustard & Brown Sugar Glaze, 98
Carrot & Apple Purée, 99
Carrots & Apricots, 99
Carrot Cake, 149
Julienne Vegetables with Lemon Butter Sauce, 90, 100
Norwegian Stir-Fry Broccoli & Carrots, 102
Pasta & Vegetables in Garlic Sauce, 76
Rainbow of Four Vegetables with Hollandaise Sauce, 101
Rye–Carrot Bread, 74
Sweet & Sour Carrots, 87, 98

Carrot & Apple Purée, 99

Carrots & Apricots, 99

Carrot Cake, 149

Cauliflower

Cauliflower Bacon Salad, 28
Cauliflower, Brie & Bacon Soup, 4
Cauliflower Crab Chowder, 4

Cauliflower Bacon Salad, 28

Cauliflower, Brie & Bacon Soup, 4

Cauliflower Crab Chowder, 4

Cheese

B.O.O.M. Quiche, 68
Brown Rice with Mushrooms, Sour Cream & Jack Cheese, 78
Cauliflower Bacon Salad, 28
Cauliflower, Brie & Bacon Soup, 4
Cheesy Potatoes, 112
Cheesy Taco Casserole, 41
Chicken Fromage, 51
Chicken with Pastrami, Spinach & Cheese, 53, 86
Chicken with Sun Dried Tomatoes & Mushrooms, 55
Fiesta Chicken, 61
Fiesta Chicken Casserole, 61
Four Cheese & Spinach Tart, 15
Galettes of Dried Beef & Provolone with Fresh Spinach Sauce, 18, 82
Gâteau Florentine, 48, 88
Greens with Jack Cheese & Toasted Walnuts with Shallot Vinaigrette, 20
Ham, Broccoli & Rice Casserole, 66
Hearts of Palm Salad, 21

"Parmesan" Potatoes, 113
Pasta Shells with Three Cheeses, 77
Pear Brie Soup, 5
Pull-Apart Cheese Bread, 75
Semi-Caesar Salad, 22
Smoked Salmon-Filled Rigatoni, 10
South of the Border Squash, 110
Spinach-Stuffed Onions, 89, 106
Strawberry & Green Salad with Sweet Garlic Dressing, 24

Cheesecake Basics, 128

Cheesy Potatoes, 112

Cheesy Taco Casserole, 41

Cherry Crisp, 145

Chicken

Chicken Casserole, 62
Chicken Fromage, 51
Chicken with Herb & Garlic Cheese, 52
Chicken with Pastrami, Spinach & Cheese, 53, 86
Chicken in Phyllo with Cream Sauce, 58
Chicken in Phyllo with Lemon & Green Onion Sauce, 59
Chicken in Puff Pastry, 60, 87
Chicken with Raspberry Vinegar Sauce, 57
Chicken Velvet Soup, 8
Crab-Stuffed Chicken Breasts, 56
Crusty Chicken Wings, 163
Fiesta Chicken, 61
Fiesta Chicken Casserole, 61
Ham & Chicken Bake with Artichokes, 64
Ham & Chicken Cannelloni, 63
Spinach-Stuffed Chicken, 54, 86
Stuffed Chicken Breast Basics, 50

Chicken Casserole, 62

Chicken Fromage, 51

Chicken with Herb & Garlic Cheese, 52

Chicken with Pastrami, Spinach & Cheese, 53, 86

Chicken in Phyllo with Cream Sauce, 58

Chicken in Phyllo with Lemon & Green Onion Sauce, 59

Chicken in Puff Pastry, 60, 87

Chicken with Raspberry Vinegar Sauce, 57

Chicken with Sun Dried Tomatoes & Mushrooms, 55

Chicken Velvet Soup, 8

Chocolate

Basic Chocolate Cake, 118
Buckeyes, 92, 156
Chocolate Chip Cookies, 155
Chocolate Crème Brûlée, 124
Chocolate Hazelnut Torte, 92, 93, 117
Chocolate Marble Bavarian Pie, 141
Chocolate Marble Cheesecake, 94, 132
Chocolate Mint Bars, 92, 160
Chocolate Praline Cake, 93, 120
Chocolate Toffee Filling for Meringue Pie Shell, 95, 135
Cookie Dough Brownies, 153

Cream-Filled Cupcakes, 151
Devil's Mousse Cake with Crème de Cacao Cream, 95, 119
Eskimo Balls, 92, 157
Marble Bundt Cake, 150
Napoleon Creams, 92, 152
Tin Roof Tart, 122
Tin Roof Tart II, 123
Warm Chocolate Cake with a Soft Heart, 92, 121
White Chocolate Strawberry Filling for Meringue Pie Shell, 95, 134

Chocolate Chip Cookies, 155

Chocolate Crème Brûlée, 124

Chocolate Hazelnut Torte, 92, 93, 117

Chocolate Marble Bavarian Pie, 141

Chocolate Marble Cheesecake, 94, 132

Chocolate Mint Bars, 92, 160

Chocolate Praline Cake, 93, 120

Chocolate Toffee Filling for Meringue Pie Shell, 95, 135

Chutney Cream, 45

Cinnamon Bread, 72

Cinnamon Twist Danish, 70, 84, 85

Classic Bavarian Cream, 140

Cocktail Buns, 72

Cookies & Bars

Almond Crescents, 156
Buckeyes, 92, 156
Chocolate Chip Cookies, 155
Chocolate Mint Bars, 92, 160
Cookie Dough Brownies, 153
Cranberry Toffee Oatmeal Cookies, 155
Eskimo Balls, 92, 157
Lace Oatmeal Cookies, 94, 159
Molasses Crisps, 154
Napoleon Creams, 92, 152
Oatmeal Shortbread, 92, 159
Peanut Butter Cookies, 154
Salted Nut Bars, 92, 157
Scroll Butter Cookies, 158

Cookie Dough Brownies, 153

Corn

Hearts of Palm & Black Bean Salad, 29, 87
Sweet & Yummy Corn Pudding, 110

Cornish Hen with Sausage & Mushroom Stuffing, 46, 82

Country French Peas, 104

Crab

Cauliflower Crab Chowder, 4
Crab Bisque, 2
Crab-Stuffed Chicken Breasts, 56
Crab-Stuffed Mushrooms, 14
Red Pepper & Crab Bisque, 3
Timbales of Crab & Spinach Mousse, 13, 88

Crab Bisque, 2

Crab-Stuffed Chicken Breasts, 56

Crab-Stuffed Mushrooms, 14

Cranberry Toffee Oatmeal Cookies, 155

Cream Puff Filling, 147

Cream-Filled Cupcakes, 151

Cream Sauce & Cream Sauce with Mustard, 45

Creamy Cabbage Packets with Bacon & Onion, 109

Creamy Cole Slaw Dressing, 35

Creamy Pasta with Ham & Broccoli, 65

Creamy Raspberry Swirl Cheesecake, 94, 130

Crème Caramel, 127

Crescent Rolls, 70, 84, 85

Crunchy Bread, 75

Crusty Chicken Wings, 163

D

Desserts

See also Cakes, Cookies, Pies

Butterscotch Crème Brûlée, 125
Cheesecakes
　Blackberry Cheesecake, 94, 131
　Cheesecake Basics, 128
　Chocolate Marble Cheesecake, 94, 132
　Creamy Raspberry Swirl Cheesecake, 94, 130
　Lemon Curd Cheesecake, 94, 133
　Sour Cream Cheesecake, 94, 129
Cherry Crisp, 145
Chocolate Crème Brûlée, 124
Chocolate Hazelnut Torte, 92, 93, 117
Classic Bavarian Cream, 140
Crème Caramel, 127
Easy Fruit Cobbler, 144
Lemon Curd, 133
Puff Pastry Pears, 91, 142
Raspberry Crème Brûlée, 126
Toasted Almond Bavarian with Raspberry Sauce, 95, 140

Devil's Mousse Cake with Crème de Cacao Cream, 95, 119

Diced Potatoes with Bacon Cream, 112

Dill Pasta Vegetable Salad, 33

E

Easy Fruit Cobbler, 144

Eggs

B.O.O.M. Quiche, 68
Egg Casserole, 67
Onion Tart, 16
Potato Salad, 34
South of the Border Squash, 110
Spinach Bacon Salad, 27
Sweet & Yummy Corn Pudding, 110
Timbales of Crab & Spinach Mousse, 13, 88

Egg Casserole, 67

Eskimo Balls, 92, 157

F

Fiesta Chicken, 61

Fiesta Chicken Casserole, 61

Fillings

Apricot Purée, 147
Blackberry Purée, 130
Cream Puff Filling, 147
Lemon Curd, 133
Lemon Filling for Meringue Pie Shell, 95, 135
Quick Pastry Cream, 147
Raspberry Purée, 130
White Chocolate Strawberry Filling for Meringue Pie Shell, 95, 134

First Course

Artichoke Cream Soup, 9
Cauliflower Crab Chowder, 4
Crab Bisque, 2
Crab-Stuffed Mushrooms, 14
Four Cheese & Spinach Tart, 15
Fried Pasta with Smoked Beef & Sun Dried Tomatoes, 17, 81
Galettes of Dried Beef & Provolone with Fresh Spinach Sauce, 18, 82
Onion Fritters, 105
Onion Tart, 16
Pear Brie Soup, 5
Red Pepper & Crab Bisque, 3
Rotini in Red Butter Sauce, 76
Salmon Napoleons with Beurre Blanc, 12, 83
Salmon Timbales with Cucumber Sauce, 11
Smoked Salmon-Filled Rigatoni, 10
Soup Under Wraps, 7, 83
Spinach Soup, 6, 83
Timbales of Crab & Spinach Mousse, 13, 88
Tomato Dill Soup, 8
Tomato Soup, 6, 83
Zucchini Bacon Soup, 9

Five Hour Stew, 40
Four Cheese & Spinach Tart, 15
French Onion Soup, 7
French Rice, 78
Fresh Mushroom Salad, 30
Fried Pasta with Smoked Beef & Sun Dried Tomatoes, 17, 81

G

Galettes of Dried Beef & Provolone with Fresh Spinach Sauce, 18, 82
Gâteau Florentine, 48, 88
Graham Cracker Crust, 116
Grain

Barley Casserole, 80

Green Bean & Almond Rice, 79, 90
Greens with Jack Cheese & Toasted Walnuts with Shallot Vinaigrette, 20
Greens & Strawberries with Poppy Seed Dressing, 25
Guacamole, 164
Guacamole Pie, 164

H

Ham

Creamy Pasta with Ham & Broccoli, 65
Ham, Broccoli & Rice Casserole, 66
Ham & Chicken Bake with Artichokes, 64
Ham & Chicken Cannelloni, 63
Ham Salad, 165

Ham, Broccoli & Rice Casserole, 66
Ham & Chicken Bake with Artichokes, 64
Ham & Chicken Cannelloni, 63
Ham Salad, 165
Hearts of Palm & Black Bean Salad, 29, 87
Hearts of Palm Salad, 21
Hollandaise Sauce, 101

J

Jelly Roll, 148
Julienne Potatoes, 111
Julienne Vegetables with Lemon Butter Sauce, 90, 100

L

Lace Oatmeal Cookies, 94, 159
Lemon

Lemon Curd, 133
Lemon Curd Cheesecake, 94, 133
Lemon Filling for Meringue Pie Shell, 95, 135
Lemon Layer Pie, 139

Lemon Curd, 133
Lemon Curd Cheesecake, 94, 133
Lemon Filling for Meringue Pie Shell, 95, 135
Lemon Layer Pie, 139

M

Main Dish

Beef

Beef Tenderloin with Mustard Balsamic Vinegar Sauce, 38
Beef with Wine Sauce, 39, 89
Cheesy Taco Casserole, 41
Five Hour Stew, 40
Stove Top Casserole, 40

Casseroles

Cheesy Taco Casserole, 41
Chicken Casserole, 62
Fiesta Chicken Casserole, 61
Pasta Shells with Three Cheeses, 77
Seafood Casserole, 47
Tex-Italian Pasta Fiesta, 42

Chicken

Chicken Casserole, 62
Chicken Fromage, 51
Chicken with Herb & Garlic Cheese, 52
Chicken in Phyllo with Cream Sauce, 58
Chicken in Phyllo with Lemon & Green Onion Sauce, 59
Chicken in Puff Pastry, 60, 87
Chicken with Raspberry Vinegar Sauce, 57
Chicken with Sun Dried Tomatoes & Mushrooms, 55
Chicken Velvet Soup, 8
Crab-Stuffed Chicken Breasts, 56
Fiesta Chicken, 61
Ham & Chicken Bake with Artichokes, 64
Ham & Chicken Cannelloni, 63
Spinach-Stuffed Chicken, 54, 86
Stuffed Chicken Breast Basics, 50

Cornish Hen with Sausage & Mushroom Stuffing, 46, 82

Eggs

B.O.O.M. Quiche, 68
Egg Casserole, 67
Gâteau Florentine, 48, 88

Ham

Creamy Pasta with Ham & Broccoli, 65
Ham, Broccoli & Rice Casserole, 66
Ham & Chicken Bake with Artichokes, 64
Ham & Chicken Cannelloni, 63

Pork

Marinated Pork Tenderloin Medallions, 43
Pork Tenderloin Tournedos, 44, 90

Marble Bundt Cake, 150
Marinated Pork Tenderloin Medallions, 43
Meringue Pie Shell, 95, 134
Molasses Crisps, 154
Mushrooms

Artichoke Cream Soup, 9
B.O.O.M. Quiche, 68
Brown Rice with Mushrooms, Sour Cream & Jack Cheese, 78
Chicken with Sun Dried Tomatoes & Mushrooms, 55
Cornish Hen with Sausage & Mushroom Stuffing, 46, 82
Crab-Stuffed Mushrooms, 14
Fresh Mushroom Salad, 30
Rainbow of Four Vegetables with Hollandaise Sauce, 101

Mustard

Baby Carrots with Mustard & Brown Sugar Glaze, 98
Beef Tenderloin with Mustard Balsamic Vinegar Sauce, 38
Cream Sauce & Cream Sauce with Mustard, 45
French Rice, 78
Pasta Salad with Mustard Dressing, 32

N

Napoleon Creams, 92, 152
Norwegian Stir-Fry Broccoli & Carrots, 102

O

Oatmeal Shortbread, 92, 159
Olives

B.O.O.M. Quiche, 68

Onions

B.O.O.M. Quiche, 68
French Onion Soup, 7
Onion Fritters, 105
Onion Tart, 16

Spinach-Stuffed Onions, 89, 106
Surprise Combination Salad, 35, 88
Sweet & Sour Carrots, 87, 98
Onion Fritters, 105
Onion Tart, 16
Orange Currant Sauce, 45
Oven Roasted Potatoes, 89, 113
Overnight Coffeecake, 71

"Parmesan" Potatoes, 113
Pasta
Cheesy Taco Casserole, 41
Chicken Casserole, 62
Creamy Pasta with Ham & Broccoli, 65
Dill Pasta Vegetable Salad, 33
Fried Pasta with Smoked Beef & Sun Dried Tomatoes, 17, 81
Ham & Chicken Bake with Artichokes, 64
Ham & Chicken Cannelloni, 63
Pasta Salad with Mustard Dressing, 32
Pasta Shells with Three Cheeses, 77
Pasta & Vegetables in Garlic Sauce, 76
Rotini in Red Butter Sauce, 76
Smoked Salmon-Filled Rigatoni, 10
Stove Top Casserole, 40
Sweet Pasta Salad, 33
Tex-Italian Pasta Fiesta, 42
Pasta Salad with Mustard Dressing, 32
Pasta Shells with Three Cheeses, 77
Pasta & Vegetables in Garlic Sauce, 76
Peach
Peach Praline Angel Cake, 144
Sweet Potato, Peach & Cashew Bake, 111
Peach Praline Angel Cake, 144
Peanut Butter
Buckeyes, 92, 156
Peanut Butter Cookies, 154
Peanut Butter Cookies, 154
Pears
Pear Brie Soup, 5
Puff Pastry Pears, 91, 142
Pear Brie Soup, 5
Peas
Country French Peas, 104
Peas with Broccoli Medallions, 104
Peas with Broccoli Medallions, 104
Pecans
Chocolate Praline Cake, 93, 120
Pecan Cream Pie, 94, 137
Pecan Cream Pie, 137, 94
Phyllo Dough
Chicken in Phyllo with Cream Sauce, 58
Chicken in Phyllo with Lemon & Green Onion Sauce, 59
Spinach Strudel, 107
Pies & Sweet Tarts
Basic Pie Crust, 116

Chocolate Marble Bavarian Pie, 141
Chocolate Toffee Filling for Meringue Pie Shell, 95, 135
Graham Cracker Crust, 116
Lemon Filling for Meringue Pie Shell, 95, 135
Lemon Layer Pie, 139
Meringue Pie Shell, 95, 134
Pecan Cream Pie, 94, 137
Pumpkin Layer Pie, 138
Strawberry Cream Pie, 94, 136
Strawberry Tart, 143
Tin Roof Tart, 122
Tin Roof Tart II, 123
White Chocolate Strawberry Filling for Meringue Pie Shell, 95, 134
Popcorn Balls, 162
Pork
Marinated Pork Tenderloin Medallions, 43
Pork Tenderloin Tournedos, 44, 90
Pork Tenderloin Tournedos, 44, 90
Potatoes
Cheesy Potatoes, 112
Diced Potatoes with Bacon Cream, 112
Julienne Potatoes, 111
Oven Roasted Potatoes, 89, 113
"Parmesan" Potatoes, 113
Potato Salad, 34
Sweet Potato, Peach & Cashew Bake, 111
Twice-Baked Potatoes, 114
Potato Salad, 34
Puff Pastry
Chicken in Puff Pastry, 60, 87
Galettes of Dried Beef & Provolone with Fresh Spinach Sauce, 18, 82
Puff Pastry Pears, 91, 142
Salmon Napoleons with Beurre Blanc, 12, 83
Soup Under Wraps, 7, 83
Puff Pastry Pears, 91, 142
Pull-Apart Cheese Bread, 75
Pumpkin Layer Pie, 138

Q
Quick Pastry Cream, 147

R
Radish Butter, 165
Rainbow of Four Vegetables with Hollandaise Sauce, 101
Raspberry
Chicken with Raspberry Vinegar Sauce, 57
Creamy Raspberry Swirl Cheesecake, 94, 130
Raspberry Crème Brûlée, 126
Raspberry Purée, 130
Raspberry Vinaigrette, 36
Raspberry Crème Brûlée, 126
Raspberry Purée, 130
Raspberry Vinaigrette, 36
Red Cabbage Salad, 30

Red Pepper & Crab Bisque, 3
Rice
Brown Rice with Mushrooms, Sour Cream & Jack Cheese, 78
Fiesta Chicken Casserole, 61
French Rice, 78
Green Bean & Almond Rice, 79, 90
Ham, Broccoli & Rice Casserole, 66
Rice with Cranberries, Green Onions & Pine Nuts, 80
Seafood Casserole, 47
Rice with Cranberries, Green Onions & Pine Nuts, 80
Romaine, Mandarin Orange & Glazed Almond Salad, 23
Rotini in Red Butter Sauce, 76
Rye–Carrot Bread, 74

S
Salads
Broccoli, Bacon & Raisin Salad, 28
Cauliflower Bacon Salad, 28
Dill Pasta Vegetable Salad, 33
Dressing
Creamy Cole Slaw Dressing, 35
Raspberry Vinaigrette, 36
Strawberry Vinaigrette, 36
Fresh Mushroom Salad, 30
Greens with Jack Cheese & Toasted Walnuts with Shallot Vinaigrette, 20
Greens & Strawberries with Poppy Seed Dressing, 25
Hearts of Palm & Black Bean Salad, 29, 8
Hearts of Palm Salad, 21
Pasta Salad with Mustard Dressing, 32
Potato Salad, 34
Red Cabbage Salad, 30
Romaine, Mandarin Orange & Glazed Almond Salad, 23
Sauerkraut Salad, 31
Semi-Caesar Salad, 22
Spinach Bacon Salad, 27
Spinach & Vegetable Salad with Chutney Dressing, 26
Strawberry & Green Salad with Sweet Garlic Dressing, 24
Surprise Combination Salad, 35, 88
Sweet Pasta Salad, 33
Wilted Cabbage Salad, 31
Salmon Napoleons with Beurre Blanc, 12,
Salmon Timbales with Cucumber Sauce,
Salted Nut Bars, 92, 157
Sauces
Beef Tenderloin with Mustard Balsamic Vinegar Sauce, 38
Beef with Wine Sauce, 39, 89
Beurre Blanc, 12
Broccoli with Orange Shallot Butter, 103
"Caramel" Sauce, 121
Chicken in Phyllo with Cream Sauce, 58
Chicken in Phyllo with Lemon & Green Onion Sauce, 59

Chicken with Raspberry Vinegar Sauce, 57

Chutney Cream, 45

Cream Sauce & Cream Sauce with Mustard, 45

Galettes of Dried Beef & Provolone with Fresh Spinach Sauce, 18, 82

Hollandaise Sauce, 101

Orange Currant Sauce, 45

Rainbow of Four Vegetables with Hollandaise Sauce, 101

Raspberry Purée, 130

Rotini in Red Butter Sauce, 76

Salmon Napoleons with Beurre Blanc, 12, 83

Salmon Timbales with Cucumber Sauce, 11

Sauces for Pork Tenderloin, 45

Toasted Almond Bavarian with Raspberry Sauce, 95, 140

Sauces for Pork Tenderloin, 45

Sauerkraut Salad, 31

Srambled Cabbage, 108

Scroll Butter Cookies, 158

Seafood Casserole, 47

Semi-Caesar Salad, 22

Smoked Salmon-Filled Rigatoni, 10

Snappy Green Beans, 105

Sorbet, 162

Soups

Artichoke Cream Soup, 9

Cauliflower, Brie & Bacon Soup, 4

Cauliflower Crab Chowder, 4

Chicken Velvet Soup, 8

Crab Bisque, 2

French Onion Soup, 7

Pear Brie Soup, 5

Red Pepper & Crab Bisque, 3

Soup Under Wraps, 7, 83

Spinach Soup, 6, 83

Tomato Dill Soup, 8

Tomato Soup, 6, 83

Zucchini Bacon Soup, 9

Soup Under Wraps, 7, 83

Sour Cream Cheesecake, 94, 129

South of the Border Squash, 110

Spinach

Chicken with Pastrami, Spinach & Cheese, 53, 86

Four Cheese & Spinach Tart, 15

Galettes of Dried Beef & Provolone with Fresh Spinach Sauce, 18, 82

Gâteau Florentine, 48, 88

Spinach Bacon Salad, 27

Spinach Soup, 6, 83

Spinach-Stuffed Chicken, 54, 86

Spinach Strudel, 107

Spinach-Stuffed Onions, 89, 106

Spinach & Vegetable Salad with Chutney Dressing, 26

Tex-Italian Pasta Fiesta, 42

Timbales of Crab & Spinach Mousse, 13, 88

Spinach Bacon Salad, 27

Spinach Soup, 6, 83

Spinach Strudel, 107

Spinach-Stuffed Chicken, 54, 86

Spinach-Stuffed Onions, 89, 106,

Spinach & Vegetable Salad with Chutney Dressing, 26

Sticky Cinnamon Rolls, 72

Stove Top Casserole, 40

Strawberries

Greens & Strawberries with Poppy Seed Dressing, 25

Strawberry Cream Pie, 94, 136

Strawberry & Green Salad with Sweet Garlic Dressing, 24

Strawberry Tart, 143

Strawberry Vinaigrette, 36

White Chocolate Strawberry Filling for Meringue Pie Shell, 95, 134

Strawberry Cream Pie, 94, 136

Strawberry & Green Salad with Sweet Garlic Dressing, 24

Strawberry Tart, 143

Strawberry Vinaigrette, 36

Stuffed Chicken Breast Basics, 50

Surprise Combination Salad, 35, 88

Sweet Pasta Salad, 33

Sweet Potato, Peach & Cashew Bake, 111

Sweet & Sour Carrots, 98, 87

Sweet & Yummy Corn Pudding, 110

Tex-Italian Pasta Fiesta, 42

Timbales of Crab & Spinach Mousse, 13, 88

Tin Roof Tart, 122

Tin Roof Tart II, 123

Toasted Almond Bavarian with Raspberry Sauce, 95, 140

Tomatoes

Hearts of Palm & Black Bean Salad, 29, 87

Onion Tart, 16

Sun Dried Tomatoes

Chicken with Sun Dried Tomatoes & Mushrooms, 55

Fried Pasta with Smoked Beef & Sun Dried Tomatoes, 17, 81

Tomato Dill Soup, 8

Tomato Soup, 6, 83

Tomato Dill Soup, 8

Tomato Soup, 6, 83

Twice-Baked Potatoes, 114

Vegetables

Baby Carrots with Mustard & Brown Sugar Glaze, 98

Broccoli with Orange Shallot Butter, 103

Carrot & Apple Purée, 99

Carrots & Apricots, 99

Cheesy Potatoes, 112

Country French Peas, 104

Creamy Cabbage Packets with Bacon & Onion, 109

Diced Potatoes with Bacon Cream, 112

Julienne Potatoes, 111

Julienne Vegetables with Lemon Butter Sauce, 90, 100

Norwegian Stir-Fry Broccoli & Carrots, 102

Onion Fritters, 105

Oven Roasted Potatoes, 89, 113

"Parmesan" Potatoes, 113

Pasta & Vegetables in Garlic Sauce, 76

Peas with Broccoli Medallions, 104

Rainbow of Four Vegetables with Hollandaise Sauce, 101

Srambled Cabbage, 108

Snappy Green Beans, 105

South of the Border Squash, 110

Spinach Strudel, 107

Spinach-Stuffed Onions, 89, 106

Sweet Potato, Peach & Cashew Bake, 111

Sweet & Sour Carrots, 87, 98

Sweet & Yummy Corn Pudding, 110

Twice-Baked Potatoes, 114

Vinegar

Beef Tenderloin with Mustard Balsamic Vinegar Sauce, 38

Beurre Blanc, 12

Chicken with Raspberry Vinegar Sauce, 57

Srambled Cabbage, 108

Snappy Green Beans, 105

Wilted Cabbage Salad, 31

Walnuts

Greens with Jack Cheese & Toasted Walnuts with Shallot Vinaigrette, 20

Strawberry & Green Salad with Sweet Garlic Dressing, 24

Warm Chocolate Cake with a Soft Heart, 92, 121

White Chocolate Strawberry Filling for Meringue Pie Shell, 95, 134

Wilted Cabbage Salad, 31

Wine or Alcohol

Apricot & Cream Sponge Layer Cake, 146

Beef with Wine Sauce, 39, 89

Beurre Blanc, 12

Cauliflower Crab Chowder, 4

Devil's Mousse Cake with Crème de Cacao Cream, 95, 119

Warm Chocolate Cake with a Soft Heart, 92, 121

Zucchini Bacon Soup, 9

Zucchini

Pasta & Vegetables in Garlic Sauce, 76

South of the Border Squash, 110

Zucchini Bacon Soup, 9